Shahnameh

The Persian Book of Kings

For Qumarss, Arash and Donya, our future generations
and the preservation of our Iranian heritage.

Our special thanks to Maryam Alaghband of the
Iran Heritage Foundation for the inspiration to sponsor this book.

P.B.

The publishers, author and illustrator would like to thank
Siamack and Parita Bagheri for their generous donation,
which made possible the publication of this book.
Our thanks are also due to Antony Wynn, linguist
and historian, and Robert Hillenbrand, former professor
of Islamic Art at Edinburgh University.

JANETTA OTTER-BARRY BOOKS

Shahnameh copyright © Frances Lincoln Limited 2012
Text copyright © Elizabeth Laird 2012
Illustrations copyright © Shirin Adl 2012

First published in Great Britain and in the USA in 2012 by
Frances Lincoln Children's Books, 4 Torriano Mews,
Torriano Avenue, London NW5 2RZ

www.franceslincoln.com

A catalogue record for this book is available from the British Library.

ISBN 978-1-84780-253-8

Set in Bembo

Printed in Shenzhen, Guangdong, China by C&C Offset Printing, Co., Ltd in December 2011

1 3 5 7 9 8 6 4 2

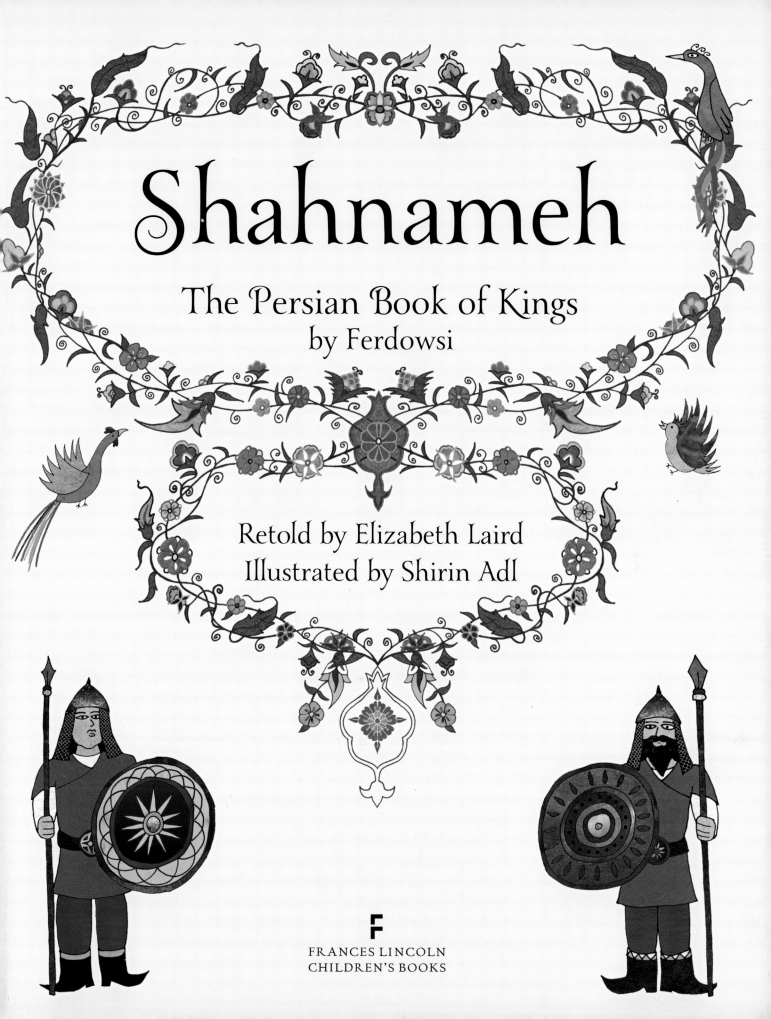

Shahnameh

The Persian Book of Kings
by Ferdowsi

Retold by Elizabeth Laird
Illustrated by Shirin Adl

F

FRANCES LINCOLN
CHILDREN'S BOOKS

Contents

For my grandson, Iskander – E.L.

For Maman and Baba – S.A.

INTRODUCTION

The Land of Stories

Iran (often known as Persia in the west) is a land of stories. There are so many that they could fill hundreds of books and take years to tell. Some of the best of them are found in the *Shahnameh*, or "Book of Kings", a very long poem which was written a thousand years ago by a great Persian poet called Ferdowsi.

People in Iran, Afghanistan, Kazakhstan and all over the mountainous lands of Central Asia know the stories of the *Shahnameh*. They have told and retold them through the centuries, from one generation to the next. Professional storytellers recite Ferdowsi's verses in tea houses by the roadside. Farmers relate them to each other as they rest in the shade of their fruit trees during the hot months of summer, and mothers and fathers tell them to their children as they huddle indoors round the fire in the cold of winter.

Iranians love to hear about what happened at the beginning of time, how the first kings ruled in glory, how the great age of heroes dawned, how champions like Sam, Zal and Rustam rode out on their fiery horses to fight wicked demons, and how brave women, like Rudabeh and Gordafarid, conquered the heroes' hearts.

I have loved these stories since I found the tale of Rustam and his son Sohrab in an old book when I was ten years old. It made me cry.

I hope you will enjoy them as much as I do.

Elizabeth Laird

AT THE BEGINNING OF TIME

Kayumars, the First King

At the very beginning of time, the first men and women who walked on the earth were the simplest creatures you can imagine. They had no clothes to wear or houses to live in. They ate their food raw, picking plums from the trees and catching fish in their hands.

There were no towns or cities then, no streets or houses, or any buildings at all. And then, one springtime, when the birds were nesting and the almond blossom was sprouting from the trees, the Great God touched a man of the mountains with divine glory, and he became the first King of Iran. His name was Kayumars, and he taught people how to eat properly and how to dress themselves, using leopard skins.

Kayumars' glory shone so brilliantly that even wild animals, large and small, the hunters and the hunted, crept and crawled and sidled to his throne and bowed down in front of him.

There was one creature, though, who hated Kayumars. He looked at him sideways through glittering eyes, as jealous as a snake. This was the devil Ahriman, and he was the fountain of everything that was cruel and ugly and evil in that beautiful, early world.

King Kayumars had a warrior son, a brave and handsome prince. But Ahriman's son was a demon, with claws like a wolf's, and fangs.

Ahriman and his son plotted and planned. They spread wicked rumours, meeting in corners and on dark nights, whispering.

Sorush the angel, the messenger of the Great God, heard of their schemes. He flew down on glittering wings. "Beware of Ahriman," he told the king. "He's gathering an army of evil followers, and they will come and attack you."

Fire flashed from the eyes of the king's son when he heard this. He prepared a great army of his own. He dressed himself in the skin of a tiger, and led his men out against the forces of Ahriman. The two armies stood and faced each other.

Then rage overcame the king's son. He ran out in front of his men, dressed only in his tiger skin, and challenged Ahriman's wolf-like son to single combat.

The cruel demon was strong and cunning. He ripped the prince to pieces with his claws and laid him dead in the dust.

Who can describe the pain of the king?
Birds hover round him on fluttering wing.
Soldiers groan, and women cry,
Hidden and fearful the animals lie.

King Hushang, the Master of Fire

King Kayumars grew old and made his grandson, Hushang, master of the world.

"You must fight the son of the demon Ahriman, who killed your father," the old king told Hushang.

A war cry rang round the land. Lions, tigers, wolves and leopards came bounding from the hills. Winged angels and fierce birds of prey swooped to answer the call. Close upon Hushang's heels, they rushed upon the trembling demon army and laid it in the dust.

From his imperial throne, Hushang began to civilise the world. He learned to forge metal and make axes and saws. He dug canals to water the land. He taught people to plant crops and harvest them.

One day, King Hushang was walking in the mountains with his men when he saw a huge snake, whose red eyes shone like fountains of blood, while black smoke billowed from its mouth. King Hushang picked up a rock and hurled it at the creature, which slid away unharmed. But the rock had struck another rock, and a shower of sparks shot out, lighting up the world. Hushang had discovered fire.

Hushang said:

> *"It is God who has sent us this great prize.*
> *Revere it and praise him, all you who are wise."*

Hushang tamed the cows, sheep and donkeys for the benefit of mankind, and showed people how to wear the skins of foxes, squirrels and sables to keep themselves warm.

At last Hushang died, and passed to a better life.

King Tahmuras, the Tamer of Animals

Hushang's son, Tahmuras, wore the girdle of glory and from him shone the splendour of a king. He learned to shear wool from the backs of sheep, to spin, weave and make cloth and carpets. He captured wild dogs and cheetahs and trained them to obey him, and he caught falcons and hawks, teaching them to fly from his wrist. He tamed roosters too, to herald the dawn.

By powerful spells and magic, King Tahmuras humbled the demon Ahriman, and rode him like a donkey. He forced the demons to teach him the art of writing: the scripts of the West, of Persia, Arabia and China.

And so he died, but his great works remained.

Jamshid the Glorious, Master of the World

Jamshid the Glorious, the son of Tahmuras, became the mightiest ruler in the world, king over other kings, ruler of the birds, the demons and the angels, for the Great God had placed in his hands power over all that lived, on earth and in heaven.

Jamshid wanted to lead his armies to victory. He learned how to forge metal and make weapons and armour: helmets, lances and chainmail. He saw that animal skins were not good to wear, so he learned to weave linen, cotton and silk. He taught his people to cut cloth and sew their clothes, so that they could look fine and beautiful for days of festival.

Jamshid separated humankind into four groups. Those who were religious went into the mountains to worship God. Those with the courage of lions became warriors who could defend the land. Those who could farm tilled the soil, living in peace and freedom, while those who could work with their hands made the crafts that people had invented.

Jamshid forced the demons to mix clay and water to make bricks, to cut stone and make mortar. They built for him tall castles, palaces and bathhouses.

Jamshid split open the rocks to find gold and silver, rubies and sapphires. He made perfumes from camphor, musk and rose-water, and medicines for the healing of wounds.

Jamshid built ships, and travelled the oceans of the world.

At last he looked on all his great works and swelled with pride.

"Build a throne for me!" he cried.

A throne was made, encrusted with priceless jewels.

"Lift me to the skies!" Jamshid ordered his demon slaves.

The demons raised the throne and flew with it to the vault of heaven. Jamshid shone there, like the sun itself, and the people on earth marvelled at him. They made the day a festival and named it Nowruz, which means "new day", and from that time to this, the people of Iran celebrate it as the beginning of the year.

Jamshid reigned for hundreds of years and the whole earth lived in peace and plenty. He discovered the secret of health and no one grew sick or died. Only the demon Ahriman resisted him, lurking secretly in a far-off lair.

But as Jamshid surveyed his own power and glory, the worm of pride entered his heart, and he said,

"Glorious Jamshid am I, above all others great.
I rule the earth and skies in my kingly state.
I ordered all the world, I made the demons flee.
Do not praise God, my people. Worship me!"

"This is not right," the people said. "The king has gone too far. He will be punished."

They were afraid and bowed their heads obediently, but in their hearts they turned away from their king. God's favour left Jamshid, and his royal power deserted him. Too late, he saw what his pride had done, and weeping tears of blood, he begged for God's forgiveness. But God had taken the gift of kingship away, and Jamshid's glory had gone for ever.

THE WICKED KING ZAHHAK

Zahhak Murders his Father

During the last years of Jamshid's rule, there lived a good and noble king in Arabia called Mirdas. Mirdas was rich and lived in a fine palace. He had a son called Zahhak.

Now, Zahhak was a foolish young man, vain, and easily led into evil ways. Observing him, the devil Ahriman saw a chance to work some wickedness. He disguised himself as a good-looking, young nobleman, and charmed his way into Zahhak's friendship, making the young prince admire and trust him.

"You poor young man," he said to Zahhak one day. "How dull it must be, waiting for so long."

"Waiting for what?" asked Zahhak, puzzled.

"Why, waiting to inherit your father's throne! Why should an old man like him live in a palace and enjoy all his splendid riches? Look at you! You're such a fine young fellow, so handsome and clever and brave, but no one thinks twice about you, while your father lords it over everyone. You should get rid of the old man, and rule in his place."

So he went on, until he turned Zahhak's weak heart to thoughts of murder.

"Leave it all to me," Ahriman said. "Soon, I promise you, your every wish will be fulfilled."

King Mirdas used to get up early in the morning, before the sun had risen, and go out into his garden to pray. The evil Ahriman, knowing this, dug a deep pit in the garden path, and covered it with branches and leaves. Mirdas fell into this cruel trap, and so he died, and Zahhak, his wicked and ungrateful son, became the King of Arabia.

Greedy Zahhak and his Loathsome Snakes

Ahriman was filled with glee at the success of his plan. Now he could go further. He disguised himself again, this time as a master cook, and presented himself at the palace.

"O King, may it please you," he said, bowing low. "I know how to make the most delicious dishes in the world. Trust me, and make me your cook."

Until that time, people had eaten only fruit, and meat was unknown to them. But Ahriman killed partridges and pheasants for the king's table, and served him lamb and veal, flavoured with saffron and rose water. Zahhak ate and ate, cramming the food into his mouth, almost fainting with pleasure. "Ask for anything you want," he said to Ahriman, "and I will give it to you."

"O King, live for ever," said Ahriman, rubbing his hands with joy. "I wish for only one thing. Allow me to kiss you on each of your royal shoulders, as if I was your friend and not your poor, humble servant."

"Is that all?" laughed Zahhak. "Why, of course!"

So Ahriman kissed each of Zahhak's shoulders, on the left and on the right, and then he disappeared, to everyone's amazement.

But from the places which his lips had touched, two vile, black snakes sprang out, writhing and hissing around Zahhak's head.

Terrified, Zahhak had them cut off, but they grew back at once. Doctors and wise men came from far and wide, but none of them could rid the king of his torment, and the snakes grew wilder and more angry.

At last Ahriman returned, disguised this time as a doctor.

"You will never be able to remove the snakes," he told Zahhak. "You must keep them calm or they will turn on you. Kill two people every day, and feed their brains to the creatures. It is the only way to save your life."

So plotted Ahriman, in his wicked heart,
To rid the world of people, by his evil art.

❧

The Death of the Great Jamshid

In Iran, where Jamshid had once ruled gloriously, there was now only chaos and turmoil. The years of peace and harmony were forgotten, and the people lived in misery. Zahhak saw his chance. He rushed across the border into Iran, attacked with a mighty army, and seized Jamshid's throne. He took for himself the Great King's palaces, his gardens and his jewels, and made Jamshid's two daughters, Arnavaz and Shahnavaz, his wives. This wicked king decreed that every day two men must die so that their brains could be fed to his snakes, but Arnavaz and Shahnavaz secretly saved as many as of the king's victims as they could.

Jamshid, once so powerful, ran for his life. For a hundred years he hid from Zahhak, but at last he was caught, and his body was sawn in half.

The great Jamshid had ruled for seven hundred years, but the evil Zahhak would rule for a thousand. Misery had come to the land. Wickedness flourished. Day after day, good men were murdered to feed the snakes that hissed on the shoulders of the king.

One night, as Zahhak lay sleeping, he dreamed a terrible dream, and woke with a shout so loud that the pillars of the palace shook, making the spiders scuttle to safety.

"What is it, husband?" asked Arnavaz, who had been sleeping beside the king.

"A warrior attacked me with a mace!" whimpered Zahhak. "He battered my head, and tied my arms and legs together, and dragged me away into the mountains!"

"Send for the wise men!" Arnavaz called to the servants. "They must interpret the king's dream."

Dark is the night as the raven's wing.
Low on his bed lies the fearful king.
The morning comes, and riding high,
The sun throws rubies at the azure sky.

The wise men approached the king, clutching each other with fear. None of them dared speak until one, braver than the others, said, "All men die, O King, and your days too will end. A child has been born who will grow into a hero, as tall as a cypress tree. He will conquer you and drag you in chains from your palace. His name is Feridun."

21

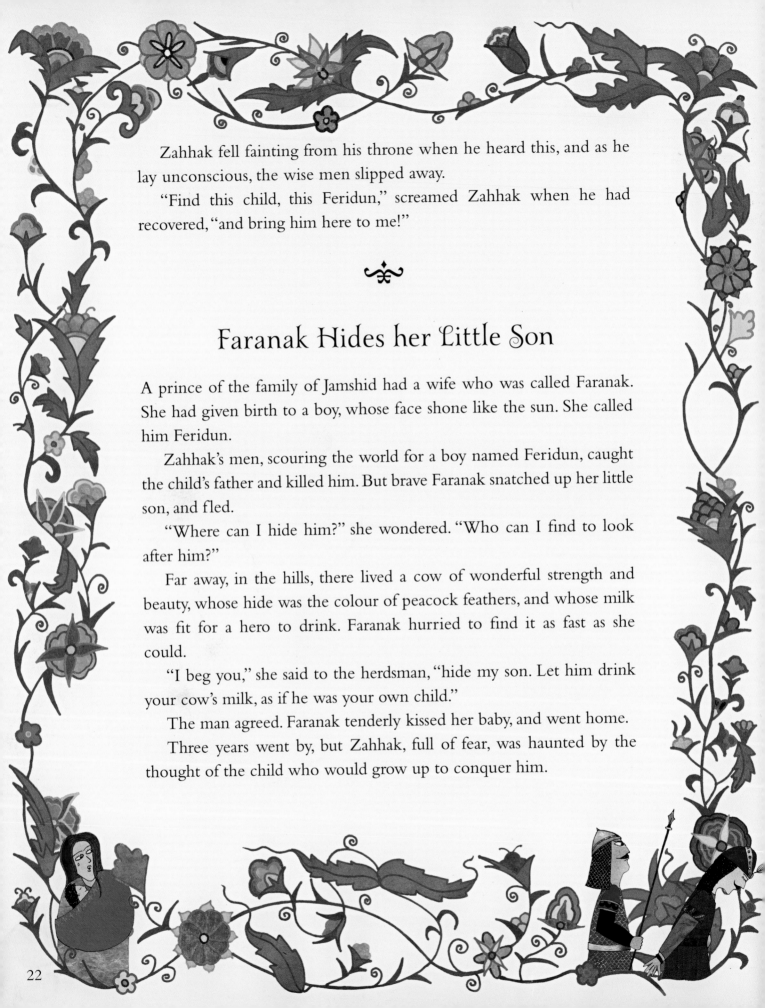

Zahhak fell fainting from his throne when he heard this, and as he lay unconscious, the wise men slipped away.

"Find this child, this Feridun," screamed Zahhak when he had recovered, "and bring him here to me!"

⁂

Faranak Hides her Little Son

A prince of the family of Jamshid had a wife who was called Faranak. She had given birth to a boy, whose face shone like the sun. She called him Feridun.

Zahhak's men, scouring the world for a boy named Feridun, caught the child's father and killed him. But brave Faranak snatched up her little son, and fled.

"Where can I hide him?" she wondered. "Who can I find to look after him?"

Far away, in the hills, there lived a cow of wonderful strength and beauty, whose hide was the colour of peacock feathers, and whose milk was fit for a hero to drink. Faranak hurried to find it as fast as she could.

"I beg you," she said to the herdsman, "hide my son. Let him drink your cow's milk, as if he was your own child."

The man agreed. Faranak tenderly kissed her baby, and went home.

Three years went by, but Zahhak, full of fear, was haunted by the thought of the child who would grow up to conquer him.

"Feridun! Feridun!" he would snarl. "Where is he hiding? I must find him. I will find him."

All he could think of was the hidden child. At last he heard of the miraculous cow grazing in her lush field.

"That is where Feridun must be!" he exclaimed.

At once he sent his soldiers to capture the little boy, but Faranak heard of his intention, and she raced like a running deer to save her son. She reached him first, snatched him up, and fled with him to the hermitage of a holy man, high up in the mountains of India.

"My son is destined to be a great king," she told the holy man. "He will defeat the monster Zahhak, who is searching for him everywhere. Hide him, I beg you, and treat him like your son."

The holy man took little Feridun, and once again Faranak had to leave him, weeping as she went.

Feridun Learns the Truth

By the time he was sixteen years old, Feridun had become a noble young man of great height and strength. Day and night, he asked the holy man to tell him about his mysterious past.

"Go to your mother," the old man said at last. "Let her tell you what you want to know."

Feridun hurried down from the mountains to his mother's royal house. "Who am I?" he asked her. "Who was my father? Why have you kept me in hiding all my life?"

"Listen, my son," answered Faranak. "Your father was a good man, descended from noble kings. The evil Zahhak murdered him, and fed his brains to the snakes which live on his shoulders. All your life, since the day of your birth, Zahhak has hunted you because of a dream that came to him long ago."

Feridun's blood boiled when he heard this. "Mother, bring my sword!" he shouted. "I will kill this monster and avenge my father!"

Faranak shook her head. "Not yet, my son," she said. "Zahhak is the ruler of the world, and has vast armies to fight for him. What can one boy do against such an enemy? Wait, till the time is right."

Feridun's rage rises high
And furious sparks flash from his eye.
Now for his father's sake he must
Lay wicked Zahhak in the dust.

❖

Kaveh, the Courageous Blacksmith

Zahhak sat hunched on his ivory throne, with his crown of turquoise pressing down on his head, brooding about Feridun, while the snakes writhed on his shoulders.

"I must be protected," he thought. "I must gather armies of men, with demons and angels in the ranks, to save me from this boy."

One day, as he sat scowling in his audience hall, there was a commotion at the door of the palace.

"I want justice!" a man was shouting. "I demand to see the king!"

"Who is it? Who's there?" asked Zahhak fearfully.

A furious man entered the audience chamber, beating his head with his hands. "I am Kaveh, the blacksmith," he called out in his deep voice. "And you, O king, are an evil tyrant! Eighteen sons I had, good men all of them. Seventeen have been sacrificed to feed your loathsome snakes, and now the last, my youngest, waits for death. What have I done to deserve this? Let my last son go! You owe me this, at least."

Zahhak listened, frightened and astonished. Then he smiled a false smile.

"You will see what a good and noble king I am," he said. "Your son is free to go. But first sign this document, which my elders have prepared, telling the world how merciful I am."

The sight of the document made Kaveh more furious than ever.

"Give that thing to me," he bellowed. "I'll show you how I'll sign it!" He snatched the document from Zahhak's hands, and tore it in two.

The king's servants and courtiers stared in wonder as Kaveh strode away to rescue his imprisoned son.

"Why did you let him go, sire?" they asked Zahhak. "No one has ever dared to speak to you like that before."

Zahhak shook his head, puzzled. "When he entered my hall," he said, "I seemed to see a mountain of iron rise up between us, and when he beat his hands against his head, I felt that my own heart was bruised."

The blacksmith's son leaps from the tyrant's cage
And the streets echo to his cries of rage,
While on the throne the serpents writhe and hiss,
Threatening Zahhak with their deadly kiss.

Outside the palace, a crowd gathered around the blacksmith and his son. Kaveh ripped off the leather apron which he wore when working in his forge, and fixed it to a lance to make a banner.

"Men of honour!" he cried. "Follow me! We'll go to Feridun. He will deliver us from the tyrant Zahhak!"

A cheer went up. The people flocked to Kaveh's leather banner. They followed him all the way to Feridun's palace, and when the young hero came out to greet them, they raised a deafening shout.

"You are the man to lead us!" they cried. "You will be our king!"

Feridun took the leather apron and decorated it with cloth of gold and sparkling jewels. On the tip of Kaveh's lance, he placed a moon-white globe. "This will be my royal banner," he declared.

A humble apron, with its leather string,
Is now the sign and symbol of a king.

Feridun Rides To War

Feridun prepared for war. He made a heavy mace shaped like the head of an ox, and put on his armour and his helmet. An army had formed around him, the warriors mounted on Arab horses, with their baggage piled on the backs of war-elephants.

They rode as fast as the wind, crossing deserts and fording rivers, until they saw in front of them Zahhak's palace, with its shining walls rising to the sky.

Full of courage, grasping his huge mace, Feridun spurred his horse through the palace gates, beating aside the powerful demons who tried to stop him.

"Zahhak!" he shouted. "Show yourself! Tyrant! Come out!"

But Zahhak, maddened by the fear of Feridun and the hissing of his snakes, was far away. He had invaded India and was rampaging through the land, slaughtering men and beasts.

So Feridun sat down on Zahhak's throne and put Zahhak's crown on his head. Zahhak's wives, Arnavaz and Shahnavaz, who were eternally young and as beautiful as ever, came out from the women's quarters. When they saw the hero, King Feridun, sitting on their husband's throne, the evil which Zahhak had planted in their hearts melted away, and they wept for joy.

"Surely, you are Feridun, the man that Zahhak feared above all others!" cried Arnavaz. "Oh, stay here! Fight the monster, and become our king!"

The Triumph of Feridun

Zahhak had a faithful servant named Kondrow. He was shocked to see his master's conqueror seated on the throne, calling for food and wine, with Arnavaz and Shahnavaz, his master's wives, by his side. He took the fastest horse from Zahhak's stables, and rode like the wind to India.

When Zahhak heard what had happened, he howled with anger like a savage wolf. Then he gathered a great army of demon warriors, and rode to take back his kingdom.

The people saw a vast cloud of dust rise up at the approach of Zahhak's army. They stood in ranks on the city walls, armed with bricks and stones, and hurled them down on the tyrant and his men. Feridun and his army attacked, and fought so valiantly that the mountains echoed to their shouts, and the earth trembled beneath their feet.

> *Stones rain down from roof and wall.*
> *Demons and heroes fight and fall.*
> *War horses rear, trampling the dead.*
> *From open wounds, the blood runs red.*

At last, Feridun felled Zahhak with a fearful blow from his ox-head mace. Then he bound the snake-shouldered monster with strips of lion hide, and sent him to live out his days, chained and alone, in a far-off cave beneath Mount Demavand.

"Give thanks to God," he told the people, "for evil has been vanquished. Put down your weapons. You have no need of them now. I promise you that I will rule justly, and show mercy to all."

When Faranak heard of her son's triumph, she bowed her head and praised God. Then she opened her family's treasure chests and secretly gave money to beggars, and the poor and needy of the land.

Good Feridun's glorious reign lasted for five hundred years, but at last, old and tired, he split his vast empire into three parts.

The lands of Rum in the west he gave to one son, China and Turkestan in the east he gave to another, and the heartlands of Iran and Arabia he gave to his youngest and favourite son, Iraj.

But Feridun's sons quarrelled bitterly over their inheritance, and none of them outlived their father. The glory of kingship passed in due time to Feridun's great-grandson, Manucher, who would rule Iran for many years.

SAM, THE FIRST CHAMPION OF KINGS

The Champion Sam
and Zal, his White-Haired Son

Feridun, the Great King, ruled over all, but under him were many lesser kings in the far-flung empire. One of these was named Sam. He was the ruler of Zabolistan, and he was the strongest, bravest and boldest warrior of all. He was known as the champion of the Great King. Whenever two armies were lined up against each other, Sam would be called forth to fight the enemy's strongest man in single combat.

Only one sorrow clouded Sam's life. He had no son. But, at last, the most beautiful of all his wives gave birth to a rosy-cheeked boy. This baby was unlike any other Iranian child, for his hair, which should have been a rich, glossy black, was as white and shining as the snow on the mountain tops.

At first, none of the women in Sam's household dared to tell the champion that his new-born son had the hair of an old man, but at last the baby's nursemaid braved his anger to bring him the news.

Sam stared scornfully down at his little son. Instead of love, he felt only anger and disappointment.

"He looks like the child of a demon!" he raged. "Anyone who sees him will laugh at me! I'll be forced to creep away in shame. Oh God, why have you punished me like this? What great sin have I committed?"

In the first flush of his fury, ignoring the pleas of the baby's mother, he commanded his men to take the child far away to the mountain of Elburz and leave him there, naked and without shelter from the burning sun, to die.

Alone and hungry the baby lies.
No one hears his feeble cries.
A stone is his pillow. Thorns make his bed.
The sun beats down on his snow-white head.

In that harsh and desolate place, where leopards roamed, a giant bird, the Simurgh, lived high up on a rocky crag. As her piercing eyes swept the valley floor, looking for prey on which to feed her chicks, she caught sight of the baby's fluttering hands.

She swooped down to snatch this promising morsel, but before her talons tore into his soft flesh, she saw how he was sucking his thumb and looking up at her with his huge, black eyes. Her motherly heart was touched. With great gentleness, she lifted him from the hot desert floor, and flew him up to her nest. She had no milk to feed him with, so he sucked the blood from the meat she gave to her chicks, who had accepted him as their brother.

In this way, Sam's abandoned son grew from year to year into a magnificent young man, who could leap from crag to crag in the high mountains, his mane of white hair flying.

❧

Sam Searches for His Son

One night, as Sam lay sleeping in his castle, he dreamed that a warrior rode out from India with news that his son was alive. Sam called for the wise men to interpret his dream.

They reproached him bitterly. "Even lions and crocodiles, and all the most ferocious wild animals, care for their children," they told him. "But you cast your son out to die in the mountains, only because of the colour of his hair. And look! Your own hair has now turned as white as milk."

Sam wept tears of shame and begged God to forgive him. Then he saddled his horse, summoned his army, and rode to Mount Elburz, where long ago he had abandoned his son.

When he reached the place, he looked up to see a massive nest, high on a rocky pinnacle, with ebony branches that seemed to nestle among the stars.

"Who could climb to such a fearful height? Oh Great God, will I never see my child again?" cried Sam, bowing so low in repentance that his face touched the ground. "Lord, help me to climb this cliff and find him!"

The Simurgh, looking down with her all-seeing eyes, saw her nestling's father, and understood at once why he had come.

"My dear child," she said to Sam's son. "Your father has come for you, and you must go back to the world of men."

The young man's eyes filled with tears. "How can I leave you?" he said to the giant bird. "Your nest is my home. You are the mother I love. I grew up sheltered under your wings."

But the Simurgh answered, "A great destiny is waiting for you. My heart breaks at the thought of losing you, but you must now go."

She pulled a feather from her breast and gave it to him. "If you are ever in danger, burn this," she said, "and I will come at once to help you. And remember me, my child, as I will always remember you." She picked him up in her huge talons, swooped down the mountainside, and set the boy gently on the ground in front of his father.

Sam gazed in awe at the handsome young giant, with his bright black eyes and flowing white hair, who was as tall as a tree and as strong as an elephant.

He thanked the Simurgh, who rose on her mighty wings and returned to her nest. Then he embraced his son and begged for his forgiveness.

"Now that I have found you," he promised, "I will never be hard-hearted towards you again. For the rest of my life, I will make sure that every one of your wishes will be fulfilled."

He named his son Zal.

Sam dressed Zal in a tunic of gold brocade, and gave him an Arab horse to ride. But as they trotted away from that desert place, Zal turned back, fixing his eyes on the great nest and the mother bird roosting there, for as long as she was in sight.

Now Zal must leave all he knows best,
His mother bird and her loving nest.
Sam cannot wait. Their journey must start.
But Zal rides away with an ache in his heart.

⊰⊱

Zal Goes Hunting

Zal was now a favoured young prince, the joy of his father's heart. When Sam went off once more to fight in the service of the Great King, Zal was free to take his friends and servants, and go hunting in the lands beyond Zabol.

At night, when the hunters' magnificent tents had been pitched, Zal called for music and wine, and the mountains and valleys echoed to the sound of riotous feasting.

The party soon came to the kingdom of Kabul. The king of this region was called Mehrab. He came from the family of the monster Zahhak of the snakes, but he was a good man, unlike his evil grandfather. Mehrab lived in peace, and paid yearly tribute to Sam, who was his overlord.

When Mehrab heard that Sam's son had entered his kingdom, he sent to the stables for his best horses, and loaded them with gifts for Zal: gold and rubies, musk and amber, cloth of gold and silk brocade, and a crown studded with jewels. Then he rode off to Zal's camp.

Zal welcomed Mehrab, and was delighted with his gifts.

'What a handsome man this king is!' thought Zal. 'He looks as brave and strong as a lion.'

'What a splendid, noble young man Zal is!' thought Mehrab. 'I wish he was a son of mine.'

As they sat and feasted together, one of Mehrab's men whispered in Zal's ear, "Did you know that Mehrab has a daughter? Her name is Rudabeh. She lives in his harem in Kabul, veiled from the eyes of men:

> *Roses bloom on her ivory cheeks.*
> *Bells chime sweetly when she speaks.*
> *The moon itself shines from her face.*
> *She is all light, and air, and charm, and grace."*

That night, when he lay down in his tent on his hard, warrior's couch, Zal could think of nothing but Mehrab's daughter. He tossed and turned till the sun rose, unable to sleep. Though he had never seen Rudabeh, he had fallen in love with her.

The next day, Mehrab came to Zal's tent, striding through the ranks of Zal's men, whose swords were sheathed in golden scabbards. "Come to my palace in Kabul and stay with me there as my guest," he said to Zal.

The smile faded from Zal's face. He searched for words, not wishing to insult the King of Kabul.

"My dear friend," he said at last. "Nothing would delight me more, but you are from the house of Zahhak, the Master of Demons. If my father hears of our friendship, he will be very angry, and so will the Great King whom he serves."

Mehrab, still outwardly friendly, but bitterly hurt in his heart, left Zal and returned to his palace in Kabul.

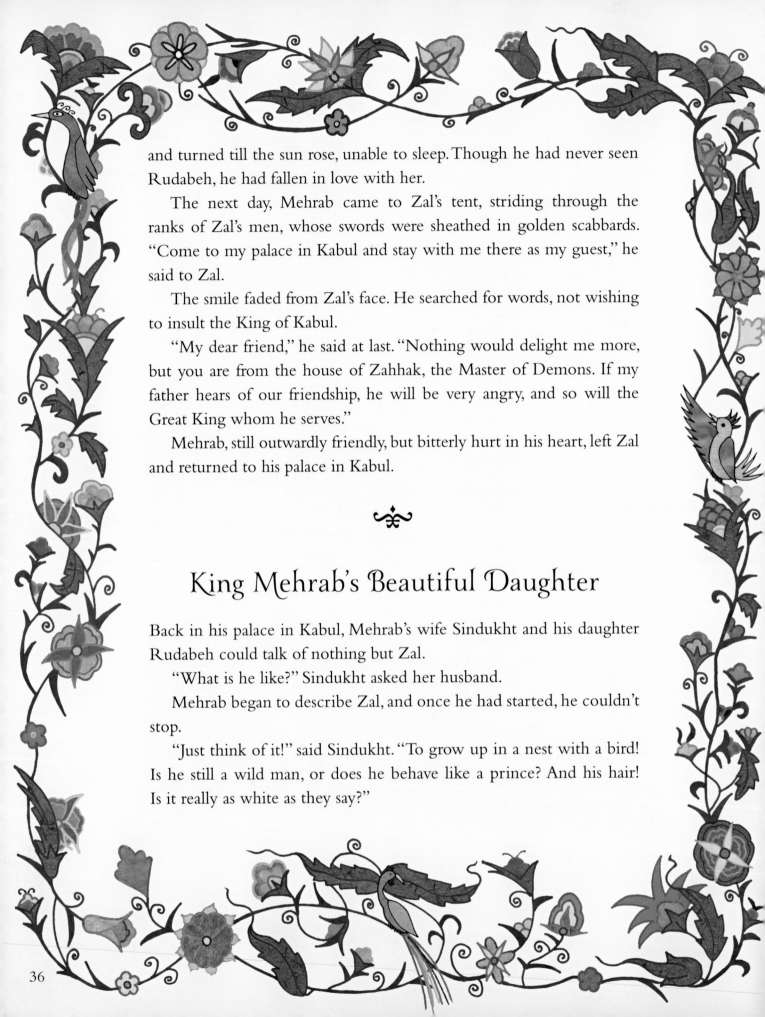

King Mehrab's Beautiful Daughter

Back in his palace in Kabul, Mehrab's wife Sindukht and his daughter Rudabeh could talk of nothing but Zal.

"What is he like?" Sindukht asked her husband.

Mehrab began to describe Zal, and once he had started, he couldn't stop.

"Just think of it!" said Sindukht. "To grow up in a nest with a bird! Is he still a wild man, or does he behave like a prince? And his hair! Is it really as white as they say?"

"He is generous," Mehrab told them. "His words are wise. In spite of his white hair, he is as handsome as an angel. And when he is in battle:

No fighter ever rode a swifter horse.
No dragon could attack with greater force."

That night, when Rudabeh lay down on the silken pillows of her bed, she could think of nothing but the hero Zal. She could not rest, but dreamed of him until the dawn broke. She had never seen Zal, but already she was in love with him.

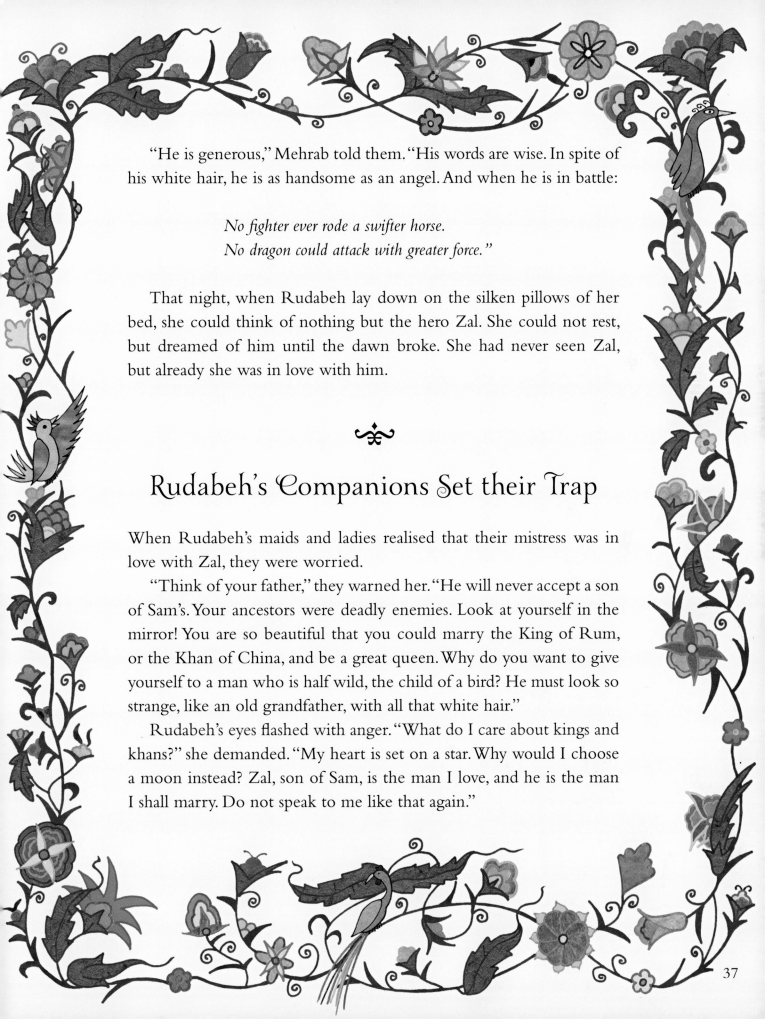

Rudabeh's Companions Set their Trap

When Rudabeh's maids and ladies realised that their mistress was in love with Zal, they were worried.

"Think of your father," they warned her. "He will never accept a son of Sam's. Your ancestors were deadly enemies. Look at yourself in the mirror! You are so beautiful that you could marry the King of Rum, or the Khan of China, and be a great queen. Why do you want to give yourself to a man who is half wild, the child of a bird? He must look so strange, like an old grandfather, with all that white hair."

Rudabeh's eyes flashed with anger. "What do I care about kings and khans?" she demanded. "My heart is set on a star. Why would I choose a moon instead? Zal, son of Sam, is the man I love, and he is the man I shall marry. Do not speak to me like that again."

Her companions saw that they could not make her change her mind. "We'll do whatever you ask," they said. "We'll fly like birds and run like deer to make your wishes come true. But be careful. Keep your love a secret, we beg you."

The maids put their heads together and made a plan. They dressed themselves in their prettiest silks, and twined roses in their hair. Then they went down to the meadow by the river, opposite the place where Zal had pitched his tents, and started to pick flowers. Their hearts beat fast, but they pretended not to notice that there were strange men on the far bank.

Zal noticed them at once. "Who are those beautiful girls?" he asked his men.

"Rudabeh's companions," someone answered.

> *Zal's heart bounds inside his breast.*
> *He straps his arrows to his chest,*
> *Picks up his bow, a man in a dream,*
> *And runs like the wind, down to the stream.*

As Zal gazed across the river at the girls, he caught sight of a duck swimming on the water. The duck took off and began to fly.

Lifting his bow, Zal shot it, and down it fell, right at the feet of one of Rudabeh's companions. "Go over and fetch it," Zal told his page.

The boy rowed across the river, and the girls clustered round him.

"Who shot that arrow?" they asked the page, although they knew the answer perfectly well. "We have never seen anyone who looks so noble and so skilful. He must be a king, at least."

"He is Zal," the boy said, "the son of the champion Sam, and there is no one to equal him in the whole world."

"Yes, there is," objected the girls. "Rudabeh, our mistress, is lovelier and more magnificent than any man. How marvellous it would be if two such people could be united! It would be like the sun marrying the moon!"

Zal's page couldn't hide his smiles. He picked up the duck, rowed back across the river, and told his master everything.

"Come with me to my treasure tent," said Zal. "I must give you presents to take back to them."

He loaded his page with gold and jewels and fine brocade, and the boy took them back across the river.

"We've caught the lion in our net!" the girls whispered to each other triumphantly when they saw the magnificent presents Zal had sent to Rudabeh.

Now it was Zal's turn to cross the river. He asked the girls to tell him more about their mistress. They praised her to the skies, and Zal's bones turned to water as he listened.

"How can I see her? How can I meet her?" he demanded.

The Falcon Catches the Dove

When Rudabeh's girls went back to the palace, their arms filled with the flowers they had gathered, the porter scowled at them.

"Where have you been, out so late, running about the countryside?" he grumbled. "It's not safe with all these foreigners camped round here. You'll be in trouble if the king sees you."

They pushed past him, and went to tell Rudabeh about Zal. They gave her the presents he had sent, and she begged them to tell her exactly how Zal had looked, and what he had said, and what they thought of him. And as they praised him, she sank back, faint, on to her cushions.

Now, Rudabeh had a pavilion of her own within her father's palace, and she hurried to make it ready for Zal's visit. She draped silks from China on the walls, set goblets of wine on golden trays, scattered jewels across the floor and filled vases with lilies, roses, jasmine and violets to scent the rooms.

When the sun went down, before the porter locked the palace gates, one of the girls slipped out to send a message to Zal.

"Come," she said. "Rudabeh is waiting for you."

His heart beating wildly, Zal ran to the palace. Looking up at the forbidding walls, he saw the loveliest face in all the world staring down at him. And Rudabeh, looking down, saw below her the handsomest man she had ever beheld.

She unbound her long hair and let it down over the wall. "Climb up my hair!" she called down to Zal.

But Zal was afraid that his weight would hurt her. Instead, he uncoiled a rope and threw it up to her, then climbed it to the top.

Zal and Rudabeh saw each other properly for the first time.

Never had two great souls fallen so much in love!
Never had such a falcon caught so sweet a dove!

They gazed and gazed at each other.

"I swear to you," said Zal at last, "that I will marry you and no one else."

"I swear the same to you," said Rudabeh. "But what shall we do? Our families hate each other. Our fathers will never agree."

"We must pray that God will help us," said Zal. "We must beg him to soften our fathers' hearts and turn their hatred into love."

❦

The Marriage of Zal and Rudabeh

Now letters flew to and fro between Zal and his father, Sam. Their bearers' horses rode so fast that sparks were struck from their hooves.

Sam, enraged at first by Zal's wish to marry Rudabeh, knew that he had to agree.

"I promised him that I would fulfil his every wish!" he said furiously. "But I never thought he would ask for anything as shameful as this. A girl from the family of Zahhak! What a calamity! The boy is as wild as his mother after all."

He sent his wise men to consult the stars.

They came back with beaming faces. "This marriage will be a good one," they said. "Zal and Rudabeh will have a son, the like of whom the world has never seen."

Sam knew then that he had to agree to the marriage of his son. At last, even Rudabeh's father, Mehrab, gave his blessing, and Zal and Rudabeh were married.

The happy couple were showered with rubies and emeralds, the banquet lasted for seven whole days and nights, and the festivities continued for a month. Then Zal and Rudabeh returned to Zabol, with a grand procession of horses and elephants, nobles and servants.

RUSTAM THE HERO

A Champion is Born

Rudabeh was expecting a child, but as the time approached for the baby to be born, she suffered so much that her cheeks, once as pink as roses, became as yellow as saffron. The child inside her seemed as mighty as iron and as heavy as stones. Rudabeh's mother, Sindukht, tried to comfort her, but Rudabeh lay fainting, unable to speak.

Zal heard of his beloved wife's distress, and he came running. As he looked down at her suffering, he was desperate with anxiety, but then he remembered the Simurgh's promise.

The fire was lit. Zal took out the Simurgh's feather and burned the edges of it in the flames. At once, the palace grew dark as the bird's giant wings covered the sky. She swooped down to land at Zal's side, and when she understood what was happening, she comforted him.

"Fetch your most skilful doctors," ordered the Simurgh. "Sharpen your best knife! Give Rudabeh wine to drink until she can feel nothing, then cut her open, and bring the lion cub out into the world."

She gave Zal another of her feathers. "Stroke the wound with this," she said. "It will heal completely."

Then she flew back to her nest far away.

They did as she had commanded, and Rudabeh gave birth to a baby boy so big, so handsome and so lusty that everyone was astonished.

Rudabeh called her son Rustam, which means 'I have been delivered'.

> *All rejoice at the marvellous birth*
> *Of a child unequalled on all the earth.*
> *Young and old, their gifts they bring.*
> *"A champion has been born!" they sing.*

❧

The Miraculous Baby

There had never been a child like Rustam. The breasts of ten women were needed to satisfy his hunger, and as soon as he was weaned he devoured enough food to feed five men. He grew so fast that by the time he was eight years old he was as tall as a cypress tree. His arms seemed to be made of iron. His legs were as strong as a mighty camel's. He had the heart of a lion and the strength of a panther.

"How like his grandfather he is!" people said. "He looks like Sam."

Sam came riding in at the head of his army to visit Zal, his son, and Rustam, his miraculous grandson. His heart was filled with joy as they feasted together.

Sam said, "Listen, Zal, and you, my grandson Rustam. Never forget to praise God, or do his will. We are a family of kings, with our own throne and kingdom here in Zabolistan, but royal glory rests on the Great King of Iran, and he is our overlord. Be his loyal champions. Fight for him whenever he calls on you. Never be tempted to do evil. Never seek riches more than honour."

Bells rang throughout the palace and drums beat as the old hero rode away once more, to serve his master, the Great King.

Rustam and the White Elephant

One night, while he was still only a boy, Rustam was woken by terrified screams.

"What is it? What's happening?" he called out.

"Your father's fiercest elephant has broken his chains, and he is on the rampage in the palace," a servant called back fearfully.

At once, Rustam leaped out of bed and ran to fetch his grandfather's ox-head mace, but when he tried to go out through the door, he found that it was bolted, and his father's men were blocking his way.

"What will Zal do to us if you're hurt?" they said. "It's dark out there. The elephant is mad with rage. His strength is legendary. He has trampled to death countless men in battle. We can't let you go out."

For an answer, Rustam felled the men with his powerful fists. He ran at the locked door, which was strengthened with iron bars, and smashed through it with one blow of his mace.

Outside, the elephant was lashing out to right and left with its mighty trunk. It towered above Rustam, so vast and powerful that, when it trumpeted, the ground shook like water boiling in a pan. Zal's soldiers huddled against the walls, as fearful as lambs in the presence of a wolf.

Rustam roared like a lion. The elephant saw him. It raised its trunk and charged. Rustam lifted the mace and hit the huge beast's head with it. The elephant stood still for a moment, trembling, then its legs buckled beneath it and it fell lifeless to the ground.

Morning came, and Sam was wakened by his quivering servants, stammering out the news of what had happened. He said:

"How many wars has this great beast won?
How many foes has he trampled down?
How could this elephant, raging and wild,
Fall to a boy who is only a child?"

Trouble Comes to Iran

The time came when the old champion Sam died. Now that the king's most heroic warrior was dead, Iran's enemies to the east, in Turan, saw their chance. The Turanian king's son, Afrasyab, was a fiery prince, mighty in battle, with great strength and cunning, and he hated the royal house of Iran like a wolf hates its hunter. He gathered a great army, stormed into Iran and placed on his own head the crown that the Great King Feridun had once worn.

In their grief and anger, the nobles and warriors of Iran tore out their hair and roared with rage. They fought against Afrasyab with all their might, and drove him back beyond the Oxus river to his own lands. But there was no strong king on the throne of Iran, and Afrasyab watched and waited, keeping his sword sharp and his armour bright. When he saw his chance he led another great army into Iran, and it was so vast that the dust it raised formed a choking cloud that blotted out the sun.

Meanwhile, Zal was no longer the white-maned boy who had once leaped from crag to crag near the Simurgh's nest. He had grown old.

The nobles of Iran came to Zabolistan to fetch him. "Why are you, the champion of the world, living here in idleness," they said, "when the enemies of Iran are attacking us?"

Zal shook his head. "In my warrior days, as you well know, there was no fighter compared to me. No enemy was safe from my sword. No army dared to stand against me. Look at me now. My back is bent with the weight of age. But I have a son! He is a lion in courage and as tall and strong as a tree. I'll find a horse that's worthy to carry him, and I'll fill his heart with anger at the misery which evil Afrasyab has brought to Iran. Rustam will drive the Turanians back to their lairs. Rustam will be your new champion!"

Zal had spoken bravely, but in his heart he feared for his son.

"You are still a boy," he said to Rustam, "and too young to be a warrior. You should be enjoying the time of your youth in feasting and music and wine. How can I send you into battle against an enemy as experienced and courageous as Afrasyab?"

Rustam replied, "Remember how I killed the elephant, Father! How can you doubt me? I don't want to lie on soft cushions and spend my days in idleness. I'm ready to be a man and go to war. God will protect me and lead me to victory. I need only a horse brave and strong enough to carry me, and a mace massive enough to crush my enemies' heads."

Zal, proud to hear his son's brave words, sent at once for Sam's huge ox-head mace and gave it to Rustam. Then he set about finding a horse worthy of the new champion.

Rustam Finds his Marvellous Horse

Zal commanded that herds of horses should be brought to him for inspection from far and wide. He made them run past Rustam so that the young hero could choose the best. Rustam picked out one after another and pressed his hands down on their backs, but each one buckled under his great strength till its belly touched the ground.

At last, a herd from Kabul galloped by. Among them was a magnificent grey mare, with ears as sharp as daggers. Behind her trotted a huge foal. He was as golden as saffron, with markings the colour of roses.

Rustam sees the golden foal trot by.
He notes the sturdy legs, the tail held high,
The mighty chest, the eyes of shining black.
This one can take a champion on his back.

Without a word, Rustam made a noose in his rope, ready to lasso the foal. But the herdsman called out to him, "Hey, master, whoever you are! Don't take a horse that doesn't belong to you!"

"Whose is he, then?" asked Rustam.

"No one knows for sure," the man answered, "but there are stories told about him already. He is known as Rakhsh. He's as quick as fire, and as bright as water. He's been ready for the past three years to saddle, but every time a horseman comes with a rope to catch him, the mother attacks like a dragon. She could rip the skin from a leopard and tear the heart from a lion."

Rustam threw his noose and caught the foal round the neck.

At once, the mare charged at him, wild as a raging elephant, ready to snatch the head from his shoulders with her powerful teeth. Rustam gave a roar and hit the mare a blow on her neck. She rolled over in the dust and lay still. But then she leaped up, and ran from him to rejoin her herd.

Rustam tightened the noose, drawing the foal closer. He pressed on Rakhsh's back with all the strength of his mighty hands, but the young horse seemed barely to feel the pressure.

"I have found you. You are the horse for me," said Rustam.

He leaped on to Rakhsh's back, and the horse raced off with the speed of the wind.

"What is the price of this young dragon?" he asked the herdsman when he had ridden back. "How much must I pay for him?"

The herdsman answered, "I can see that you are Rustam himself. Take the foal. His price is the land of Iran which you will rescue with his help. Together, you will save us."

Rustam laughed, and thanked God for the gift of Rakhsh. He saddled him, and began to train him. Zal, seeing that his son had found a horse of such wisdom and spirit, was filled with joy. He knew that Rustam and Rakhsh would perform great marvels in the service of Iran.

Rustam Seeks a King

What now could stop the young hero from leading an army out against the cruel Afrasyab? Only the chills of winter.

Spring came at last, and it was now the season of flowering roses. Zal called for war. Then the drums and trumpets, the Indian bells and the feet of trampling elephants made a din as loud as the Day of Judgement, when the earth will cry out to the dead, "Rise up!"

When Zal and Rustam had led their army close to the place where Afrasyab was camped, Zal called the nobles together.

"Listen, heroes of Iran!" he said. "Our army is strong. Our battle plan is good. But there is something we lack, which will bring all our hopes to nothing. We need a king. A prince from the family of Feridun, who is strong and wise enough to sit on the throne of his ancestors and wear the girdle of kingship. And I know of just such a man. He is tall, gracious, full of majesty, courtesy and judgement. His name is Kay Kobad."

He turned to Rustam and said, "Take your mace, my son. Hurry to the Elburz mountains. Find Kay Kobad and bring him here so that we can place the crown of Iran on his head."

Rustam bowed in obedience, vaulted on to Rakhsh's willing back, and turned the horse's head towards the mountains. As he rode, the outposts of Afrasyab's army tried to block his way, but he beat them aside with his mace. They crawled back to their king complaining of the massive hero who had sent them sprawling. As Afrasyab listened, he frowned and chewed his lip.

Rustam rode on in his quest until, in the foothills of the mountains, he came to a grove of trees beside a clear stream of water. A golden chair was set there, and on it sat a young man whose face glowed like the moon. Ranks of nobles stood about him.

When they saw Rustam approach, they called out hospitably, "Come and join us, friend! Drink wine with us! Be our guest!"

"Thank you, my lords," answered Rustam, "but my quest is too urgent for delays. Iran is overrun by her enemies. There is grief and mourning in every home, while the throne of Feridun stands empty, needing a king."

"If you need to go further, we'll escort you," the young men said. "We know these mountains well. But first tell us what you're looking for."

"I seek a prince of royal blood, called Kay Kobad," said Rustam. "Do you know where I can find him?"

The man seated on the golden chair smiled. "I know Kay Kobad," he said. "Dismount, and sit beside me. I'll tell you about him."

Rustam jumped from Rakhsh's back and sat beside the young man, in the shade of the lush trees beside the stream, and drank the cup of wine that was offered to him.

"Tell me," the young man said. "Why are you looking for Kay Kobad?"

"My father is Zal, the champion of the king," answered Rustam. "He has sent me to find Kay Kobad, and take him to Iran, so that he can sit on the throne and be our king."

"Your quest is ended. I am Kay Kobad," the young man said, gazing in astonishment at Rustam. "Last night, I dreamed that two white falcons flew out from Iran towards me, holding a shining crown in their beaks. They placed it on my head. This dream filled me with such hope that I gathered my nobles here. Then you came, Rustam, like a falcon, offering, as your gift, the crown of Iran."

Rustam and Kay Kobad leaped on to their horses, and rode for Iran, not stopping by day or by night. When they reached Zal's army, they feasted and rejoiced for seven days, and on the eighth day Kay Kobad took his place on the ivory throne, and the crown of Iran was placed on his head.

There in the glade beside the spring
Rustam bows before his king.
Warriors shout. Musicians play.
Iran's dark night breaks into day.

The Noble Kay Kobad

Kay Kobad was a noble king, and Rustam was his strong right arm. Together, they chased the cunning Afrasyab back to his own land of Turan across the Oxus river, and peace and justice reigned in the world.

Kay Kobad ruled for a hundred years, and he grew old. He chose from among his sons Kay Kavus to be the new king.

The passing years were as nothing to Rustam. He was a young man still, handsome, strong and vigorous. He was the champion of the world.

The Musician of Mazanderan

Kay Kavus was not like his father. When he grasped the emerald crown and saw that a great empire lay at his feet, and when his father's Arab horses were paraded before him with their flowing manes, pride filled his heart.

An evil demon saw his chance. Disguised as a musician, he came to the garden where Kay Kavus sat sipping wine, surrounded by his lords.

"Sing!" commanded the king. "Amuse us!"

The demon began to strum his lyre and sing:

> *My country is Mazanderan,*
> *Bliss it is, for beast and man!*
> *Springtime lasts for ever,*
> *Snow and frost come never!*

Kay Kavus listened, his mouth open, and a dreadful ambition entered his heart.

"Look at us!" he burst out, scowling at his warriors. "Here we sit, idling our time away. Lolling about on cushions! You know who I am – the most powerful of all kings! Greater than Jamshid, and Zahhak, and my father, and all who have come before me. But I need to prove my strength and courage. We will invade this wonderful country of Mazanderan, and take its pleasures for ourselves."

His courtiers and generals were shocked.

"This is folly," whispered the noble Tus. "Mazanderan is the kingdom of the devils and the home of the White Demon, the most powerful of them all."

"You are right," answered the courageous Gudarz. "The King of Mazanderan rules by magic and sorcery. Not even the great Jamshid or the mighty Feridun tried to wage war against him."

His son, brave Giv, agreed. "We would never come out of Mazanderan alive," he said.

But none of them dared to speak out.

"There's only one hope," they told each other. "We must send for wise Zal. No one else can persuade the king to abandon this disastrous plan, which must have come from the mind of Ahriman, the master of evil."

A messenger was despatched to Zal, begging him to come. Zal shook his head when he heard of the folly of Kay Kavus, but he travelled as fast as he could to the royal court. Still dusty and tired from his journey, he went straight to the garden where the king was sitting. He bowed low, and greeted Kay Kavus tactfully, praising his power and glory. Slowly, cautiously, he began to speak of Mazanderan.

"There is no sword, however sharp, which can break the magic of the demons," he told the king. "No warrior could be found, however brave, who could fight an invisible magician. Your men are soldiers. They will obey you, but they are God's children too. Do not waste their lives in this venture, sire, I beg you."

But Kay Kavus refused to listen. "You will see, old man," he said. "Mazanderan will be mine, the demons will be wiped off the face of the earth, and my name will blaze brighter than that of any king before me. If you and your son will not share in this glory, stay here at home."

Zal saw that no words would sway the king. He set out sadly for his home in Zabolistan. Tus, Gudarz and Giv watched him go, shaking their heads over the folly of their king.

The White Demon of Mazanderan

As soon as Zal had gone, Kay Kavus ordered his generals Tus and Gudarz, with Giv, Gudarz's son, to prepare for war. Drums beating and flags flying, the vast Iranian army marched to Mazanderan. They camped in the mountains, in a shaded place haunted by demons, where even the elephants feared to go. Kay Kavus spread cloths of gold on the ground, and he and his lords feasted all night long.

In the morning, Kay Kavus said to Giv, "Choose your best men. Go and take Mazanderan. Burn every house. Kill everyone you find, both old and young. Let us cleanse the world of demons."

Reluctantly, Giv did as he was commanded. His men spread the misery of death and destruction, and it was as if they were pouring poison on to the land.

When they came to Mazanderan, they found that it was as beautiful as a dream. Gold and jewels were piled in every corner. The women were dressed in silks of China, and they were as lovely as the maidens of Paradise.

A week passed, while the Iranians looted the conquered land. But then news of the invasion reached the King of Mazanderan.

"Run fast," he told a servant. "Faster even than the sun in its journey across the sky. Tell the White Demon what has happened. If he does not come to help us, not a single living thing will remain in Mazanderan."

The White Demon growled when he heard the news, and rose to his feet. He was as huge as a mountain, and his head seemed to touch the spinning stars.

When night came, a thick cloud blotted out the army of Iran. Stones and javelins began to rain down out of the dense black fog. Dawn broke at last, and when the cloud lifted, Kay Kavus found that he was blind. Most of his soldiers, too, had lost their sight, while their treasure chests had been spirited away. They were captives.

"Oh, why did I not listen to Zal?" cried Kay Kavus.

Then came the voice of the White Demon, echoing as loud as thunder from hill to hill. "You proud and foolish king! Did you not know what I could do? You have brought all this upon yourself."

He put the Iranian prisoners in chains, set demons armed with daggers to guard them, and retreated to his lair in the mountains.

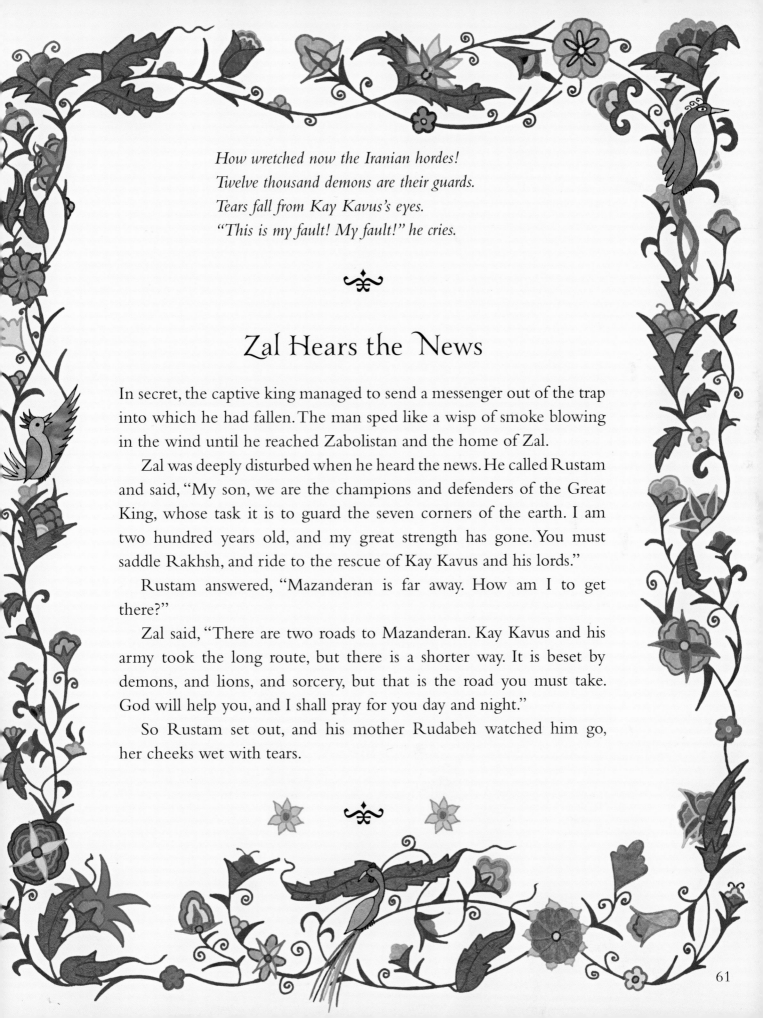

How wretched now the Iranian hordes!
Twelve thousand demons are their guards.
Tears fall from Kay Kavus's eyes.
"This is my fault! My fault!" he cries.

Zal Hears the News

In secret, the captive king managed to send a messenger out of the trap into which he had fallen. The man sped like a wisp of smoke blowing in the wind until he reached Zabolistan and the home of Zal.

Zal was deeply disturbed when he heard the news. He called Rustam and said, "My son, we are the champions and defenders of the Great King, whose task it is to guard the seven corners of the earth. I am two hundred years old, and my great strength has gone. You must saddle Rakhsh, and ride to the rescue of Kay Kavus and his lords."

Rustam answered, "Mazanderan is far away. How am I to get there?"

Zal said, "There are two roads to Mazanderan. Kay Kavus and his army took the long route, but there is a shorter way. It is beset by demons, and lions, and sorcery, but that is the road you must take. God will help you, and I shall pray for you day and night."

So Rustam set out, and his mother Rudabeh watched him go, her cheeks wet with tears.

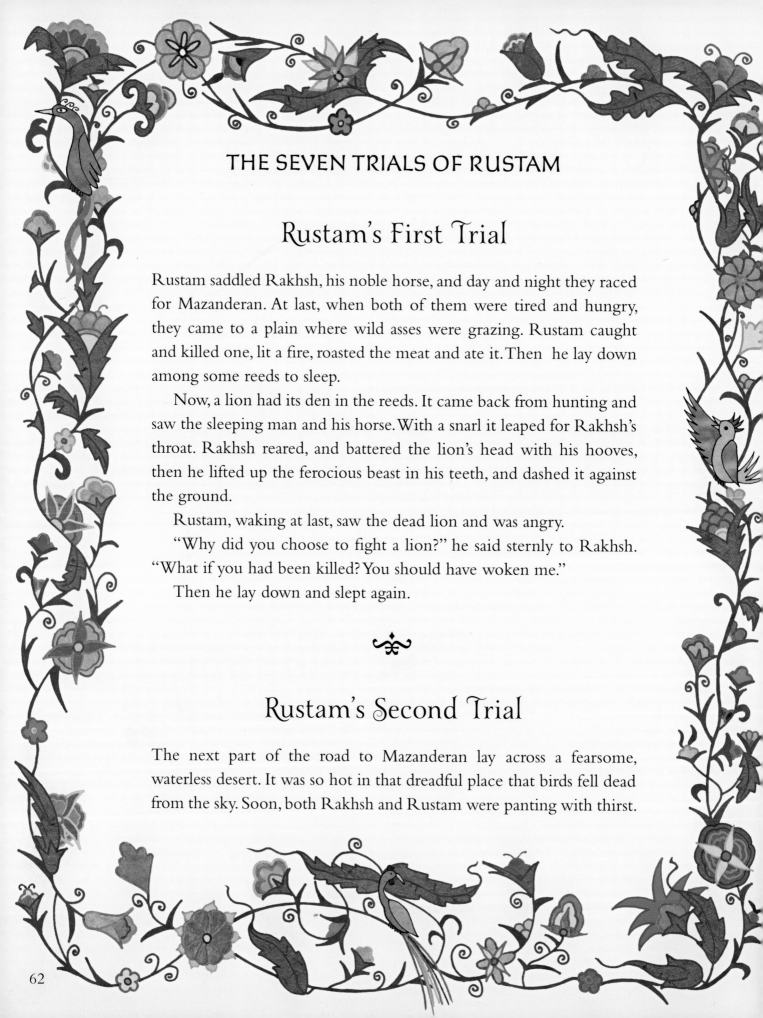

THE SEVEN TRIALS OF RUSTAM

Rustam's First Trial

Rustam saddled Rakhsh, his noble horse, and day and night they raced for Mazanderan. At last, when both of them were tired and hungry, they came to a plain where wild asses were grazing. Rustam caught and killed one, lit a fire, roasted the meat and ate it. Then he lay down among some reeds to sleep.

Now, a lion had its den in the reeds. It came back from hunting and saw the sleeping man and his horse. With a snarl it leaped for Rakhsh's throat. Rakhsh reared, and battered the lion's head with his hooves, then he lifted up the ferocious beast in his teeth, and dashed it against the ground.

Rustam, waking at last, saw the dead lion and was angry.

"Why did you choose to fight a lion?" he said sternly to Rakhsh. "What if you had been killed? You should have woken me."

Then he lay down and slept again.

Rustam's Second Trial

The next part of the road to Mazanderan lay across a fearsome, waterless desert. It was so hot in that dreadful place that birds fell dead from the sky. Soon, both Rakhsh and Rustam were panting with thirst.

Rustam saw how weak Rakhsh had become, so he dismounted and continued on foot, stumbling at every step. In despair, he prayed aloud:

"O Great God, who rules on high,
Look down on me and hear my cry.
The king lies captive far away
In the demons' cruel sway.
Only I can set him free.
O Great God, look down on me!"

And he fell to the burning ground, and lay helpless and exhausted.

At that very moment, a sheep came wandering by.

'Where there are animals, there must be water,' thought Rustam. He felt a new hope, and staggered to his feet. Leading Rakhsh by the bridle, he followed the sheep and came to a spring of sparkling water, surrounded by lush grass. They both drank deeply, until they were refreshed. Then Rustam hunted down another wild ass and when he had eaten it, he lay down to sleep, with Rakhsh grazing peacefully beside him.

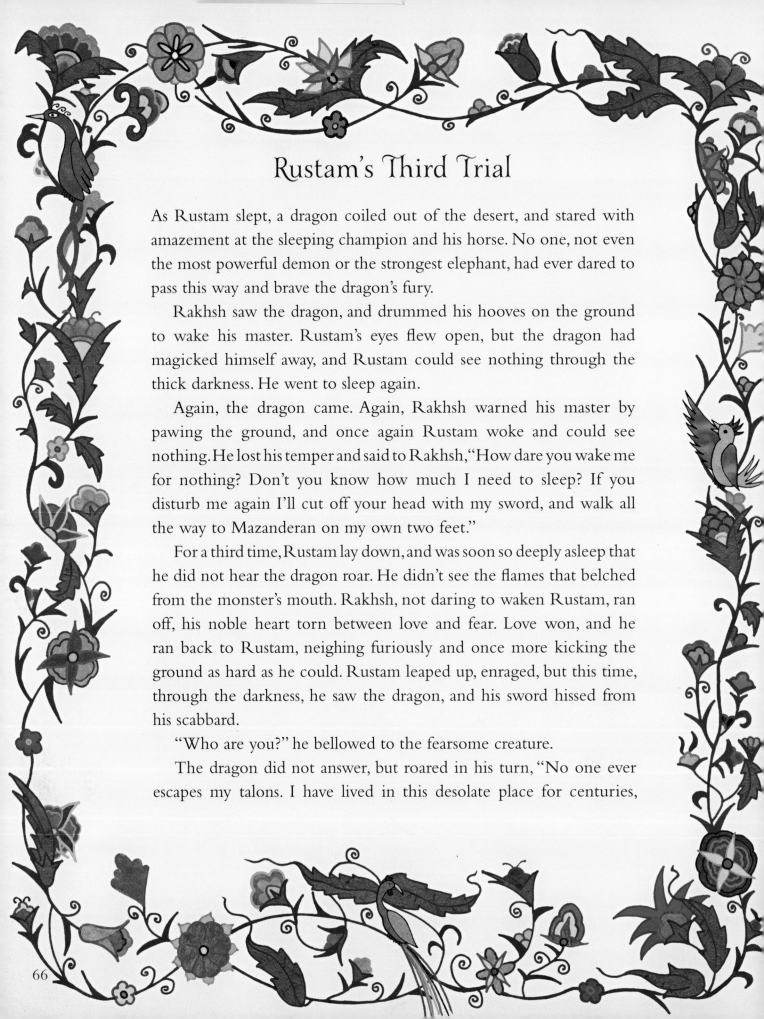

Rustam's Third Trial

As Rustam slept, a dragon coiled out of the desert, and stared with amazement at the sleeping champion and his horse. No one, not even the most powerful demon or the strongest elephant, had ever dared to pass this way and brave the dragon's fury.

Rakhsh saw the dragon, and drummed his hooves on the ground to wake his master. Rustam's eyes flew open, but the dragon had magicked himself away, and Rustam could see nothing through the thick darkness. He went to sleep again.

Again, the dragon came. Again, Rakhsh warned his master by pawing the ground, and once again Rustam woke and could see nothing. He lost his temper and said to Rakhsh, "How dare you wake me for nothing? Don't you know how much I need to sleep? If you disturb me again I'll cut off your head with my sword, and walk all the way to Mazanderan on my own two feet."

For a third time, Rustam lay down, and was soon so deeply asleep that he did not hear the dragon roar. He didn't see the flames that belched from the monster's mouth. Rakhsh, not daring to waken Rustam, ran off, his noble heart torn between love and fear. Love won, and he ran back to Rustam, neighing furiously and once more kicking the ground as hard as he could. Rustam leaped up, enraged, but this time, through the darkness, he saw the dragon, and his sword hissed from his scabbard.

"Who are you?" he bellowed to the fearsome creature.

The dragon did not answer, but roared in his turn, "No one ever escapes my talons. I have lived in this desolate place for centuries,

and not even the eagles dare to fly over it. Now you must tell me your name, for soon your mother will be weeping over your dead body."

"My name is Rustam. I am the son of Zal who is the son of Sam," said Rustam, "and even on my own I am as strong as an army. You will soon see, for I am going to send your head rolling in the dust."

Now the dragon rushed at Rustam, and so furious was his attack that for a while it seemed that he would win. But Rakhsh, seeing the danger his master was in, laid back his ears and launched himself at the dragon, biting the great beast's shoulders. Then Rustam was able to slice off the dragon's head with a single blow, and the blood flowed out in torrents.

Rustam, astonished by his horse's courage and devotion, gave thanks to God for his victory. Then he washed himself in a nearby stream, saddled Rakhsh and went on his way towards the country of the sorcerers.

Rustam's Fourth Trial

Rustam rode fast all day, and when evening came he arrived at a stream of clear, cool water, by which grew flower-studded grasses and rustling trees. A meal was laid out all ready for a hero to eat. There was roast meat and bread, sweet dishes and a goblet brimming with wine.

Rustam dismounted. He sat down and helped himself to the wine. Then he saw a lute lying there. He began to strum it, and sang this song:

> *"Rustam am I, a champion bold,*
> *Feared by the wicked, the young and the old.*
> *I have no pillow to cradle my head,*
> *The desert's my home; stones are my bed.*
> *Crocodiles hide at the sight of me.*
> *Lions tremble and tigers flee."*

A sorceress, hiding nearby, heard Rustam's music. She disguised herself as a young girl with a face as lovely as springtime. She walked up to the champion, her brightly coloured clothes floating around her, her perfume filling the air, and sat down beside him.

Rustam, amazed and delighted, poured a cup of wine for her, and gave thanks to God for His goodness. But at the name of God, the wicked sorceress flinched, her face darkened, and she became hideously ugly. Rustam leaped to his feet, threw his noose and caught her. Drawing her close to him, he commanded, "Show me who you really are!"

She shrank down, crumpled and twisted, and there in front of him was an old witch, full of wickedness. He drew out his dagger, and cut her in half.

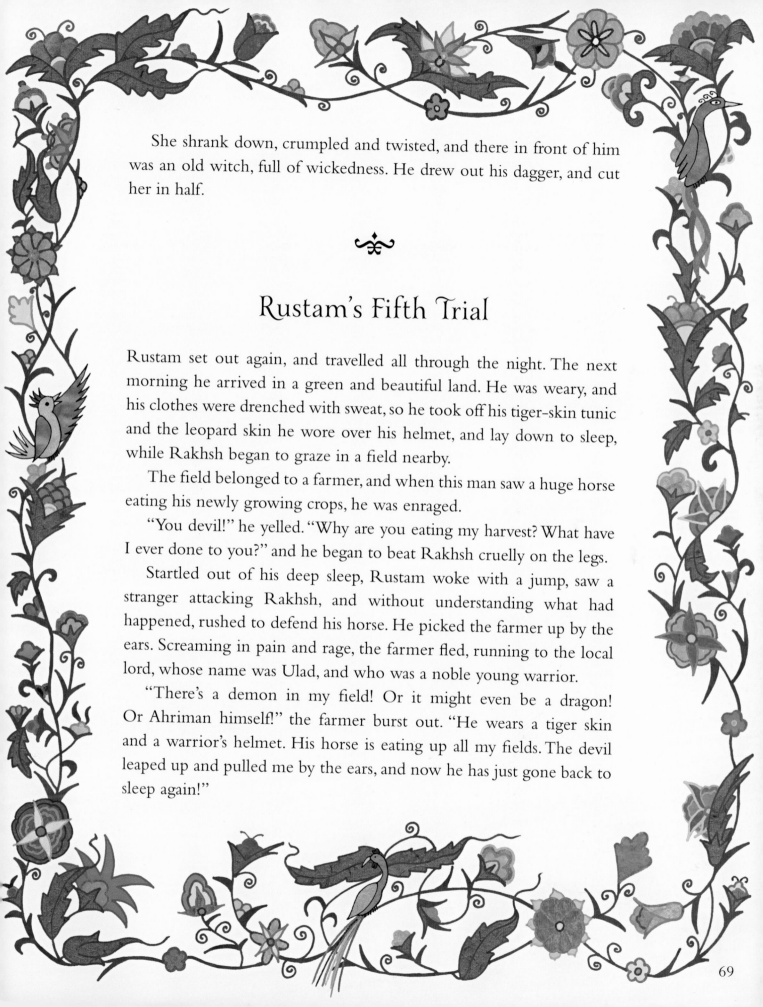

Rustam's Fifth Trial

Rustam set out again, and travelled all through the night. The next morning he arrived in a green and beautiful land. He was weary, and his clothes were drenched with sweat, so he took off his tiger-skin tunic and the leopard skin he wore over his helmet, and lay down to sleep, while Rakhsh began to graze in a field nearby.

The field belonged to a farmer, and when this man saw a huge horse eating his newly growing crops, he was enraged.

"You devil!" he yelled. "Why are you eating my harvest? What have I ever done to you?" and he began to beat Rakhsh cruelly on the legs.

Startled out of his deep sleep, Rustam woke with a jump, saw a stranger attacking Rakhsh, and without understanding what had happened, rushed to defend his horse. He picked the farmer up by the ears. Screaming in pain and rage, the farmer fled, running to the local lord, whose name was Ulad, and who was a noble young warrior.

"There's a demon in my field! Or it might even be a dragon! Or Ahriman himself!" the farmer burst out. "He wears a tiger skin and a warrior's helmet. His horse is eating up all my fields. The devil leaped up and pulled me by the ears, and now he has just gone back to sleep again!"

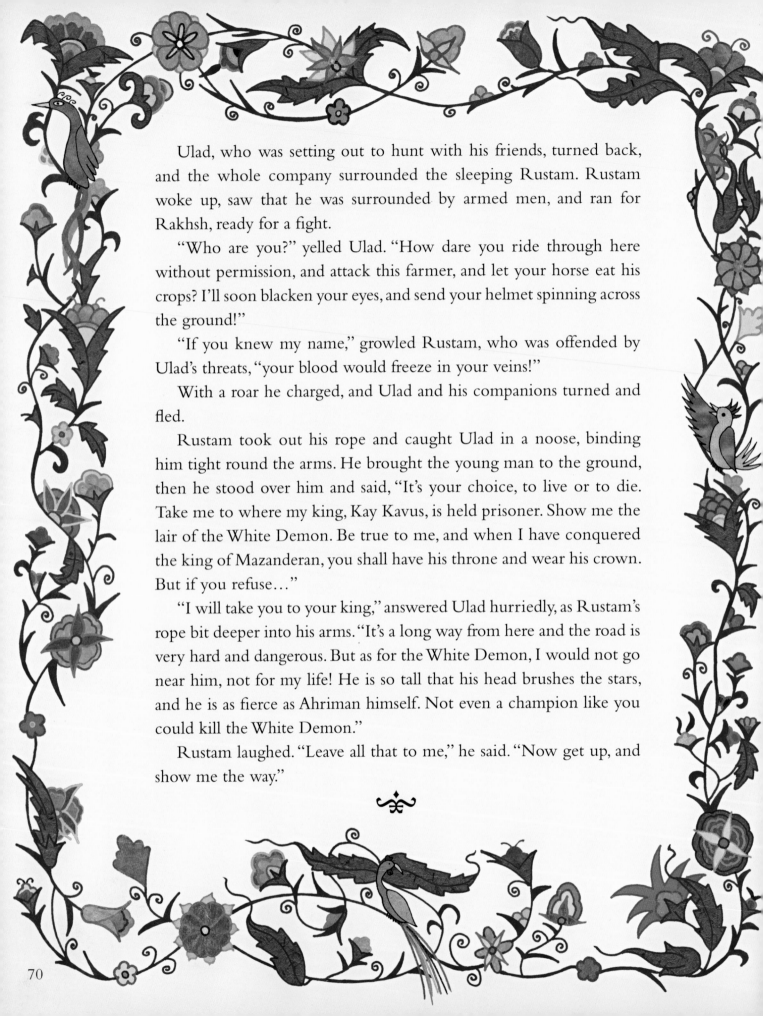

Ulad, who was setting out to hunt with his friends, turned back, and the whole company surrounded the sleeping Rustam. Rustam woke up, saw that he was surrounded by armed men, and ran for Rakhsh, ready for a fight.

"Who are you?" yelled Ulad. "How dare you ride through here without permission, and attack this farmer, and let your horse eat his crops? I'll soon blacken your eyes, and send your helmet spinning across the ground!"

"If you knew my name," growled Rustam, who was offended by Ulad's threats, "your blood would freeze in your veins!"

With a roar he charged, and Ulad and his companions turned and fled.

Rustam took out his rope and caught Ulad in a noose, binding him tight round the arms. He brought the young man to the ground, then he stood over him and said, "It's your choice, to live or to die. Take me to where my king, Kay Kavus, is held prisoner. Show me the lair of the White Demon. Be true to me, and when I have conquered the king of Mazanderan, you shall have his throne and wear his crown. But if you refuse…"

"I will take you to your king," answered Ulad hurriedly, as Rustam's rope bit deeper into his arms. "It's a long way from here and the road is very hard and dangerous. But as for the White Demon, I would not go near him, not for my life! He is so tall that his head brushes the stars, and he is as fierce as Ahriman himself. Not even a champion like you could kill the White Demon."

Rustam laughed. "Leave all that to me," he said. "Now get up, and show me the way."

Rustam's Sixth Trial

Rustam rode on, with Ulad running as fast as the wind in front of him. Night fell. Through the darkness, they could see fires flickering here and there, and the noise of distant drums.

"We are entering the land of Mazanderan now," Ulad told Rustam. "The great demon Arzhang must be nearby. There is always a noise where he is."

Rustam, undismayed, halted, and the two of them slept till dawn. Then Rustam, having tied Ulad to a tree to prevent his escape, rushed to the tent where the demon Arzhang stayed, and killed him with his mace. All the other demons fled, leaving the way clear to Mazanderan.

Rustam Finds the King

By this time, Kay Kavus and his men had been prisoners for so long that they had lost hope of ever being rescued. Blind and helpless, they were sunk in despair. Then, one glad morning, the king heard the sound of Rakhsh neighing in the distance.

"I know that horse!" he said, starting up. "It's Rakhsh! Rustam has come!"

His men shook their heads. "The poor king has lost his mind," they whispered. "All this sorrow has been too much for him."

But at that very moment, Rustam burst in among them and knelt in front of the blinded king. As the Iranian nobles, with Tus, Gudarz and Giv among them, crowded round, putting out their hands to feel who was there, Kay Kavus pulled Rustam to his feet and asked him all the news from home.

Then he said, "Rustam, there is one more great deed that you must perform. Slip out of here, before the demons guarding us see you, and fly at once to the cave of the White Demon. He must be destroyed, or he will bring disaster on us all. The way is hard. You must cross seven mountains, with demons on all sides, and the cave itself is guarded by more cruel monsters, who are as fierce as tigers. When you have killed the White Demon, bring us some of his blood, because a few drops of it will cure us of our blindness."

Rustam's Seventh Trial

Rustam and Ulad set out, and at last they came near to the White Demon's cavern, a vast black hole in the mountainside guarded by armies of lesser demons. Rustam pulled Rakhsh up, and said to Ulad, "You have been faithful and true to me. You overcame your fear to bring me to this place. Do one more thing for me. Tell me how I can defeat the White Demon."

"These evil demons are awake all night," answered Ulad, "but when the sun rises they fall into a deep sleep. That is the moment to attack."

Rustam waited impatiently, and when he saw that only a few guards were left awake, he drew out his dagger and ran at them, his roar louder than a roll of deafening thunder, and he scattered them to right and left.

At the entrance to the White Demon's lair Rustam paused, peering inside, but the cavern was like the mouth of Hell, very deep and dark, and he could see only a little way in.

Screwing up his eyes, he went inside, his sword in his hand, and saw at last the monstrous body of the White Demon, so huge that it filled the entire cave. Rustam roared again. The White Demon woke, shook its horrid head, picked up a boulder and rushed at Rustam, ready to crush him.

And so the battle began. The demon and the hero slashed and stabbed at each other, reeling backwards and forwards across the blood-drenched floor of the cave.

'If I get out of this alive,' Rustam thought, 'I will never fear anything again.'

'If I survive,' thought the White Demon, 'I will have to hide my wounds in shame for ever more.'

At last, Rustam gathered himself for one last effort. He lifted the huge bulk of the demon up in his mighty arms and dashed it to the ground, then he plunged his dagger into the wicked creature's heart.

So dies the demon, Rustam's evil foe,
Felled by the hero, with one mighty blow.

Rustam tore out the demon's liver, which was filled with blood, so that he could cure the king and his men of their blindness.

As he and Ulad rode back to Kay Kavus, Rustam said to Ulad, "I promised that I would make you the king of Mazanderan, when all these evil demons had been conquered, and you can be sure, noble Ulad, that I will keep my word."

Ulad Wins his Kingdom

When Rustam and Ulad returned to the prisoner king, a shout of joy went up from all the Iranian nobles. Rustam poured drops of the White Demon's blood into their eyes, and at once they could all see again, as brilliantly as if the sun had risen after the darkest night.

Now that the White Demon was dead, and the Iranian nobles were freed, Kay Kavus could lead his men against the Demon King of Mazanderan, a savage-faced monster, with the tusks of a wild boar curling out from his face.

Long and hard was the war against this evil being. The Demon King transformed himself first into a vast boulder, and then into a black cloud, but at last Rustam defeated him and led the Iranians to victory. The demons' cruel reign over Mazanderan was over.

In his gratitude, Kay Kavus heaped treasures on Rustam. He gave him a throne made of turquoise, a royal crown studded with jewels, garments made of cloth of gold, a hundred menservants and a hundred maidservants. He gave him a hundred horses richly caparisoned, a hundred mules with golden bridles, a ruby cup filled with perfume, a turquoise cup filled with rose-water and a document written on silk. And he granted him the lordship of rich lands.

He praised Rustam to the skies, but Rustam said, "Sire, you must thank Ulad, who showed me the way. I promised him the throne of Mazanderan, and he has earned it by his courage and faithfulness."

And so Ulad became the wise and just ruler of Mazanderan, and Kay Kavus and the armies of Iran returned to their own country. Bells rang, drums thundered, trumpets blared and all the people sang for joy.

Home to his father Rustam goes.
He has served his king and slain his foes.
Peace now reigns over all Iran.
So ends the tale of Mazanderan.

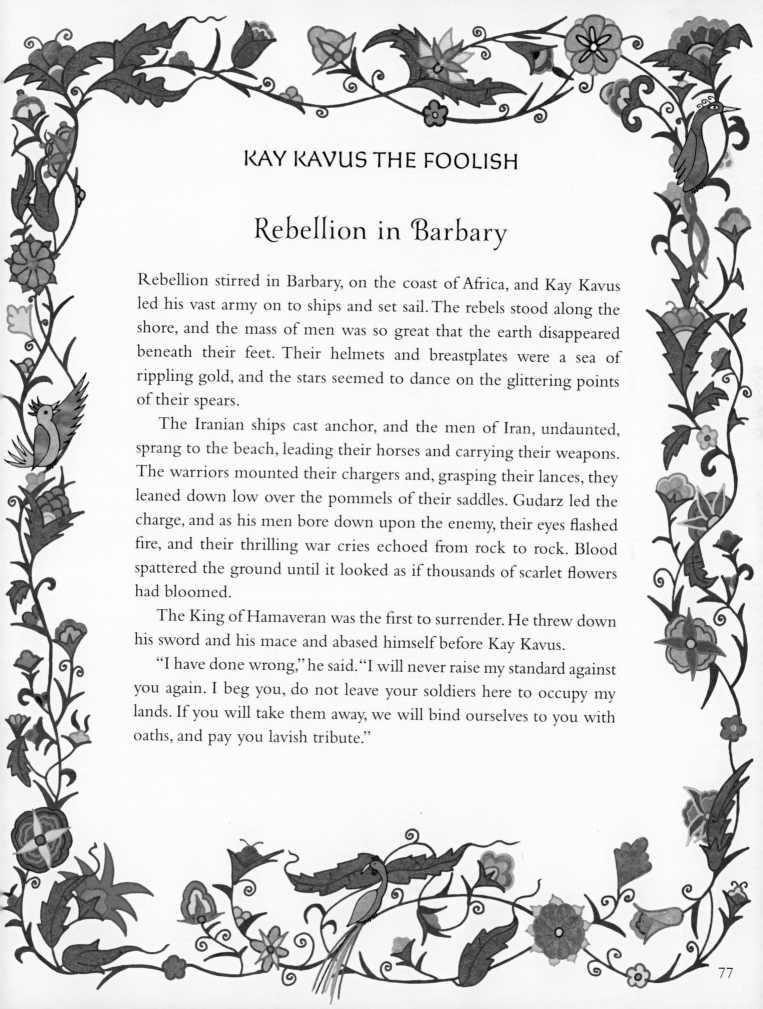

KAY KAVUS THE FOOLISH

Rebellion in Barbary

Rebellion stirred in Barbary, on the coast of Africa, and Kay Kavus led his vast army on to ships and set sail. The rebels stood along the shore, and the mass of men was so great that the earth disappeared beneath their feet. Their helmets and breastplates were a sea of rippling gold, and the stars seemed to dance on the glittering points of their spears.

The Iranian ships cast anchor, and the men of Iran, undaunted, sprang to the beach, leading their horses and carrying their weapons. The warriors mounted their chargers and, grasping their lances, they leaned down low over the pommels of their saddles. Gudarz led the charge, and as his men bore down upon the enemy, their eyes flashed fire, and their thrilling war cries echoed from rock to rock. Blood spattered the ground until it looked as if thousands of scarlet flowers had bloomed.

The King of Hamaveran was the first to surrender. He threw down his sword and his mace and abased himself before Kay Kavus.

"I have done wrong," he said. "I will never raise my standard against you again. I beg you, do not leave your soldiers here to occupy my lands. If you will take them away, we will bind ourselves to you with oaths, and pay you lavish tribute."

"I agree," said Kay Kavus. "From now on, you are under my protection. Your enemy is my enemy and there is no more quarrel between us."

He returned to his tent, and messengers from the King of Hamaveran brought to him tributes of gold, emeralds and suits of armour.

"We are the dust beneath your feet," they told Kay Kavus.

The King of Hamaveran's Daughter

Someone whispered in the ear of Kay Kavus that the King of Hamaveran had a daughter, hidden in his harem, whose lips were as sweet as sugar, who wore her beautiful black hair like a royal crown and who was as merry as the spring-time sun. Her name was Sudabeh.

Kay Kavus's heart leaped at this news. He called for his wisest courtier. "Go to the King of Hamaveran," he told the man. "Tell him that I want to marry his daughter. Sing my praises. Tell him of my glory, my greatness, how the world lies at my feet, and so forth. He's sure to be honoured and delighted. Where, after all, would he find a son-in-law like *me*?"

The courtier hurried to obey.

The King of Hamaveran listened to Kay Kavus's message with a polite smile on his lips, but his heart was filled with bitterness.

'Kay Kavus has everything!' he thought. 'He is the master of us all, and we lesser kings run to do him homage. But I have only one child, my daughter, who is dearer to me than life itself. How can I bear to lose her?'

He could not hide his sorrow from Kay Kavus's envoy. "Your master takes everything from me!" he cried. "I have given him all my wealth and now he wants my daughter! But what choice do I have? I will ask the girl, and if she agrees, I suppose the king must have her."

The princess Sudabeh was a wise young woman, who understood her tempestuous father. "But this is a high honour, Father dear," she said. "You should be happy to see me married to the greatest ruler in the world."

And so the marriage was agreed upon. Broken-hearted, the King of Hamaveran prepared a magnificent procession, with six hundred slaves, a thousand camels, a thousand mules and a thousand horses, all laden with gold and silk brocade. Sudabeh herself was carried to Kay Kavus in a sumptuous litter. The King of Hamaveran's soldiers were dressed in coloured robes so brilliant that they looked like a field of tulips.

When this great procession arrived at Kay Kavus's camp, Sudabeh stepped out of her litter and the king saw her for the first time. He stood still, awestruck by her beauty. Then he called the sages and the wise men, and the king and the princess were married with much ceremony.

The King of Hamaveran Takes his Revenge

The King of Hamaveran was outwardly all smiles, but in his heart he raged bitterly over the loss of his daughter Sudabeh, and plotted to bring her home again.

'I will invite Kay Kavus to a banquet,' he thought. 'He will suspect nothing, and will come without any weapons. I'll do what I want with him, and recover my kingdom, my riches and my daughter.'

The invitation was sent to the place where Kay Kavus was still encamped with his army.

Sudabeh understood at once what her father meant to do. "Don't go," she begged her husband. "My father will kill you, I know he will. And it will all be because of me."

But Kay Kavus refused to listen to her. "They are all cowards in this country," he told her arrogantly. "Look how your father's soldiers ran away when my cavalry charged at them. Your father would not dare to lay a hand on me."

And so he set off for his father-in-law's palace, with Tus, Gudarz, Giv and all the captains of his army as his escort.

The King of Hamaveran had prepared a banquet so splendid that the Iranians' last suspicions were stilled. They were showered with gifts of pearls and rubies, and sweet perfumes were poured on their heads. For seven days they feasted on delicious food, and drank the finest wines. But all that time, the armies of Barbary were massing outside the palace walls. On the seventh night, when the Iranians were unarmed and sated with wine, bugles sounded the attack. Kay Kavus, Tus, Gudarz and Giv, along with all the captains, were seized and tightly bound.

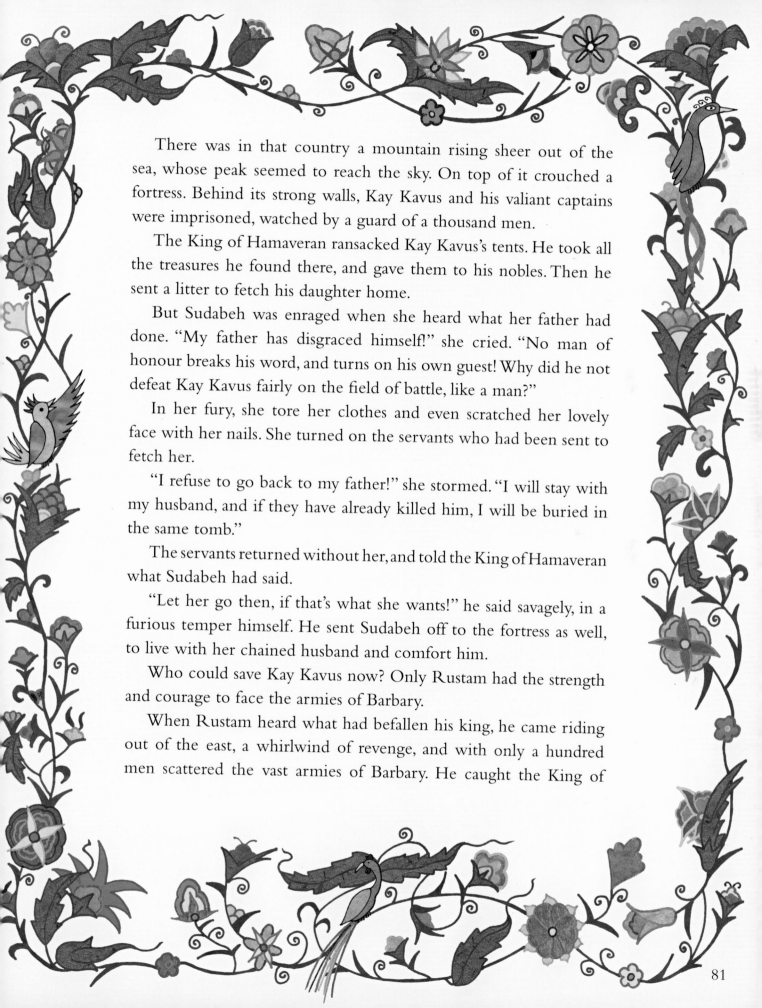

There was in that country a mountain rising sheer out of the sea, whose peak seemed to reach the sky. On top of it crouched a fortress. Behind its strong walls, Kay Kavus and his valiant captains were imprisoned, watched by a guard of a thousand men.

The King of Hamaveran ransacked Kay Kavus's tents. He took all the treasures he found there, and gave them to his nobles. Then he sent a litter to fetch his daughter home.

But Sudabeh was enraged when she heard what her father had done. "My father has disgraced himself!" she cried. "No man of honour breaks his word, and turns on his own guest! Why did he not defeat Kay Kavus fairly on the field of battle, like a man?"

In her fury, she tore her clothes and even scratched her lovely face with her nails. She turned on the servants who had been sent to fetch her.

"I refuse to go back to my father!" she stormed. "I will stay with my husband, and if they have already killed him, I will be buried in the same tomb."

The servants returned without her, and told the King of Hamaveran what Sudabeh had said.

"Let her go then, if that's what she wants!" he said savagely, in a furious temper himself. He sent Sudabeh off to the fortress as well, to live with her chained husband and comfort him.

Who could save Kay Kavus now? Only Rustam had the strength and courage to face the armies of Barbary.

When Rustam heard what had befallen his king, he came riding out of the east, a whirlwind of revenge, and with only a hundred men scattered the vast armies of Barbary. He caught the King of

Hamaveran in his noose, and forced him to release Kay Kavus and his lords. He took back the treasure which the King of Hamaveran had taken, and much more besides.

Kay Kavus chose a gentle mare to carry his bride home to Iran. He made a comfortable litter for her, and placed it on a saddle encrusted with precious stones. She travelled beside him, veiled from the view of men. And so Kay Kavus and his bride returned to Iran.

❦

Kay Kavus Flies with the Eagles

For a time, the world was quiet. Kay Kavus ruled in majesty. He was generous and just to all who lived in his realms. There was such harmony that even wolves and lambs lay down in peace together.

Angels and men served the king joyfully, but the demons gnashed their teeth in fury, for Kay Kavus forced them to work day and night. He made them carve stables for his horses out of solid rock. He made them build a pleasure dome of crystal, embedded with emeralds, where wise men could live and study. He made them build a palace of gold, where the air was scented, and spring reigned all the year round, and wine fell from the sky instead of rain. Exhausted by their labours, the demons had no time to plot their wickedness.

But one day, the devil Iblis called together a council of demons.

"This king is making our lives miserable. One of us must disguise himself as a man, and become the king's friend, and bring about his downfall," he said.

The cowardly demons looked uneasily at each other. They were all afraid of Kay Kavus. But at last one, braver than the others, stepped forward.

"I will go," he said.

This demon disguised himself as a charming and handsome young nobleman, and presented himself at Kay Kavus's court. Soon enough, through soft words and flattery, he turned the king's heart so that Kay Kavus lost all his sense, and would listen to no one else.

"Oh my lord," this cunning demon said to the king. "Such splendour and majesty shines from you, such power and glory, that you should be reigning not only on earth, but in heaven. You are the ruler of the world! You are the shepherd, and we people are your sheep!"

Kay Kavus nodded happily, and reached for another peach.

"But there is one thing that you have never accomplished," the demon went on.

"What's that?" Kay Kavus asked sharply.

"How dare the sun hide his secrets from you?" said the demon. "Not even your gracious majesty knows how he rises in one place and sets in another. You don't understand the journeys of the moon, and why night is different from day. The whole earth lies at your feet, but if you could conquer the heavens, your name would live forever."

From now on, Kay Kavus could think of nothing but the conquest of the skies. By day he paced about his palace. By night, he lay sleepless on his bed.

Kay Kavus called his wise men and asked them how far it was from the earth to the sky and the moon. He pondered their answers, and made a decision.

First, he sent men by night to raid the nests of eagles and to steal their chicks. He fed the chicks with roasted meat, and even entire lambs, so that they became as strong as lions.

The king ordered a throne to be made from wood and gold. He attached lances to the sides of the throne, and had juicy joints of lamb stuck on the tips. Then he chose the four most powerful eagles, and strapped them to the throne.

"At last!" cried Kay Kavus, "I will conquer the skies!"

He seated himself on the throne, a cup of wine in his hand, and the eagles, hungry, and maddened by the smell of meat, which was just out of their reach, flapped their wings frantically in their efforts to seize it. Powered by the huge birds, the king's throne rose up, higher and higher, until it disappeared into the clouds.

Some men say that Kay Kavus flew to heaven itself, where the angels lived. Others say that he fought against the sky with his arrows. Who knows the truth, but God?

At last, however, the eagles were exhausted. Their beating wings failed, and down and down they fell, out of the thunderous clouds, dropping like stones. Miraculously, Kay Kavus survived his fall.

The forest where Kay Kavus had landed was deep and dark, and no one knew where to find him among the thickly growing trees.

Tus, Gudarz and Giv searched for him everywhere. They were angry with their foolish king.

"Our king is good for nothing!" they all said.
"There is no sense inside his silly head.
He's weak and selfish, a mere fool;
Vain as a peacock, stubborn as a mule."

At last news came to them of where Kay Kavus could be found, and they travelled far into the forest to fetch him out. When they had found him, Gudarz reproached him bitterly.

"It's one thing after another!" he grumbled. "First you invade Mazanderan, and all of us are captured, then you trust your enemy, the King of Hamaveran, and we are thrown into prison again. Now you have even pitted yourself against Heaven! For pity's sake, Sire, ask forgiveness from God, and humble yourself before him."

Kay Kavus was deeply ashamed. At home again in his palace, he lay face down on the ground, and kept himself in seclusion for forty days, repenting of his pride and folly.

God heard the king's prayers, and Kay Kavus was forgiven. He sat once more on his throne, and peace reigned throughout his realm.

THE STORY OF RUSTAM, AND SOHRAB HIS SON

Rustam Loses Rakhsh

Rustam woke one day with a strange sadness weighing down his heart. 'I'll go hunting,' he thought, 'and try to forget this sorrow that has come over me.'

He strapped on his belt, filled his quiver with arrows, and mounting Rakhsh, galloped off towards the Turanian frontier.

Near a town called Samangan he came to a lush plain, where herds of wild asses were grazing. Loosing his bow, he shot one, then he lit a fire and pulled up a tree, as easily as if he were lifting a feather, to make a spit. He roasted the ass on the spit, ate all the meat, and lay down to sleep, leaving Rakhsh to graze nearby.

While Rustam lay sleeping, a group of Turanian horsemen trotted past. They caught sight of Rakhsh.

"What a huge, noble horse!" they said to each other. "Let's catch him. We'll take him home to Samangan and give him to our king."

They chased Rakhsh out of the reeds, where he had been grazing by the river, and one of them, unleashing his noose, caught Rakhsh round his golden neck.

Rakhsh fought valiantly, kicking out with his massive hooves and biting all within reach, but the Turanians' ropes bit into him harder and harder as they tightened, and at last he was overcome, and his enemies led him away to a stall in the King of Samangan's stables.

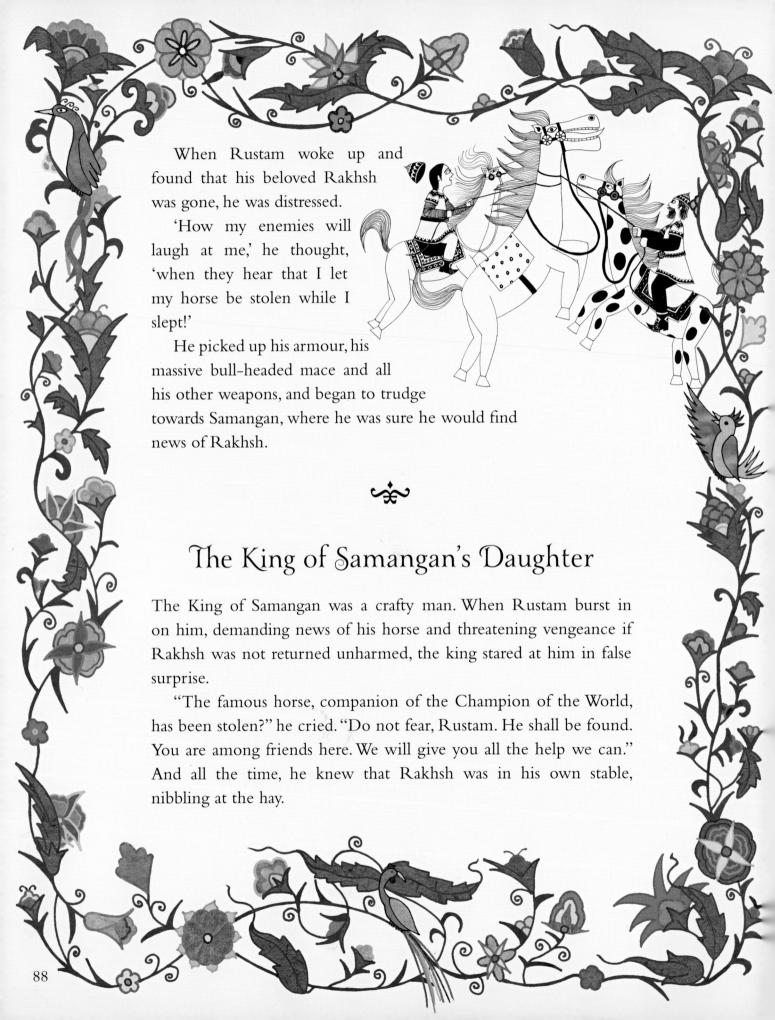

When Rustam woke up and found that his beloved Rakhsh was gone, he was distressed.

'How my enemies will laugh at me,' he thought, 'when they hear that I let my horse be stolen while I slept!'

He picked up his armour, his massive bull-headed mace and all his other weapons, and began to trudge towards Samangan, where he was sure he would find news of Rakhsh.

The King of Samangan's Daughter

The King of Samangan was a crafty man. When Rustam burst in on him, demanding news of his horse and threatening vengeance if Rakhsh was not returned unharmed, the king stared at him in false surprise.

"The famous horse, companion of the Champion of the World, has been stolen?" he cried. "Do not fear, Rustam. He shall be found. You are among friends here. We will give you all the help we can." And all the time, he knew that Rakhsh was in his own stable, nibbling at the hay.

Rustam answered, "If you can find Rakhsh for me, I will be grateful." He frowned. "But if he is not found, I will send the heads of your lords spinning from their shoulders!"

The king answered soothingly and invited Rustam to stay in the palace. He gave the hero delicious food to eat and good wine to drink, and called for beautiful young women to entertain him with their singing. And so the evening went joyfully by, and Rustam and the king went to their beds to sleep.

Tahmineh

Sometime after midnight, when the morning star was already rising in the sky, soft whispers could be heard outside Rustam's room. The door opened quietly and in came a servant, carrying a lamp. She was followed by a woman of great beauty, with lips as red as rubies, and eyes as bright as diamonds.

Rustam woke up and stared at her in astonishment.

"Who are you?" he said. "Why have you come here, in the middle of the night?"

The girl said, "My name is Tahmineh, and I am the only daughter of your host, the King of Samangan. My family is a proud one, a race of heroes and warriors. I have never been alone with a man before, and none have heard my voice until this moment. You know nothing of me, but since I was a child, I have listened to wonderful stories about you. I know that lions and leopards creep away in terror when they see you, that not even the eagle dares to swoop on its prey when you are nearby, and that the very air trembles at the slashing of your sword. And this is what I wish for – to marry you, and bear you a son. If you agree to this, I know that Rakhsh will be returned to you."

Rustam listened, amazed, but when he saw that Tahmineh was filled with grace and was as lovely as an angel, he agreed to marry her, and sent her servant at once to fetch her father.

Now, the land of Samangan was in the domain of Turan, and the king of Samangan's overlord was Rustam's old enemy, Afrasyab. When Tahmineh's father heard what his daughter had done, he thought to himself, 'This marriage could be good for us. There is sure to be war again soon between Turan and Iran, but if Rustam is in charge of the Iranian army, and invades, he won't attack his own wife and her family. He will lead his army by another way, and we in Samangan will be spared from his fury.'

And so he agreed to his daughter's request, and the marriage was performed at once. When the ceremony had been performed, the king, with his servants and sages, left the couple to themselves.

When the sun rose, hurling his brilliant shafts of light from the high vault of the sky, Rustam took from his upper arm a clasp decorated with onyx, famed throughout the world as Rustam's jewel, and gave it to Tahmineh.

"Take it," he said. "If the child you will bear is a girl, bind her hair with it, and if it's a boy, let him wear it on his upper arm, as I have done, so that everyone will know whose son he is."

The King of Samangan hurried to his son-in-law with the glad news that Rakhsh had at last been found. Then Rustam kissed Tahmineh and said goodbye to her, for he was not made to be a husband, living quietly by his wife's side. And Tahmineh, knowing this, let him go, hiding her tears.

Rustam rode like the wind for Iran, thinking all the time about what had happened, but telling no one of his marriage to Tahmineh.

> *Tahmineh has her heart's desire.*
> *She caught the hero with her eyes of fire.*
> *But now she weeps, for though she is his wife*
> *She'll never play a part in Rustam's life.*

The Birth of Sohrab

Nine months later, Tahmineh gave birth to Rustam's son, a wondrous boy, handsome and big and strong, like his father. Tahmineh named him Sohrab.

Sohrab grew with miraculous speed. When he was only three years old, he was playing polo, and by the time he was ten there was no one who dared to fight against him.

Sohrab wondered why he was so different from the other boys.

He went to his mother and said, "Why am I bigger and taller than all my friends? Who is my father? Why do you never talk about him?"

Tahmineh had been waiting for this moment. "Your father is the hero Rustam," she told her son. "He is the greatest champion in the world. Your great-grandfather was Sam the Mighty, and your grandfather is Zal the White-Haired, the foster-son of the Simurgh."

Sohrab swelled with pride at this news.

"Look," said Tahmineh, opening her casket of jewels and showing Sohrab a set of rubies encased in gold. "When your father heard of your birth, he sent these jewels for you. But listen, my brave son. You must tell no one who you really are. Afrasyab, our overlord, is your father's bitterest enemy. If he hears that Rustam has a son, he will come here and kill you, to punish your father. And if Rustam learns how big and strong you are, he will send for you to fight at his side, although you are so young, and this will break your mother's heart."

But Sohrab scowled at his mother.

"Why didn't you tell me this before?" he said fiercely. "How can I possibly keep this secret? I want my father to know me and admire me. I'm going to build up a huge army of Turanians, and attack Iran, and drive that stupid king Kay Kavus from his throne. There's only one man great enough to wear the crown of Iran, and that's my father. And when I've made him king, I'm going to invade Turan and tip Afrasyab off his throne and shake my lance at the sky. And I'll make you the queen of Iran beside Rustam. I'll show them all that I'm braver than anyone. I will not let anyone else reign anywhere in the world except for my father. All other kings are like pale stars beside his sun, and my moon."

Although he was still only twelve years old, Sohrab's fame had already spread so far that soldiers flocked to his banner. But before he could ride off to war, Sohrab needed a horse fit to carry him. Just as his father had done, he tried out one after another, but all of them buckled under the pressure of his hand.

At last, he found a horse whose sire was the son of Rakhsh himself. This noble creature had the strength and courage of a lion, and could run like the wind. Sohrab leaped on to its back, grasped his lance and cried, "No one can stand against me now! The world will soon grow black before Kay Kavus's eyes!"

His grandfather, the King of Samangan, was so impressed by his young grandson's courage that he opened his treasure house and gave Sohrab gold and weapons and horses, to help him on his campaign.

Afrasyab Plots and Plans

Afrasyab, the overlord of Sohrab's family, and the great enemy of Iran, soon heard of the extraordinary boy whose strength and courage startled all who saw him. His spies had told him of Rustam's secret marriage to Tahmineh, and in his heart he brooded on how he could use Rustam's son to his advantage.

When he heard that Sohrab had gathered an army, and was about to attack Iran, he rubbed his hands gleefully.

"You know what will happen?" he said to Houman and Barman, his generals. "When that fool Kay Kavus hears that an army has invaded from Turan, he'll send Rustam out to defeat it. Rustam will ride out in front of the Iranian army, and Sohrab will lead out the Turanians. Father and son will meet on the battlefield, but neither of them will recognise each other. Rustam is old now, but he is still the greatest warrior alive. Only one person can bring him down, and that's the cub which the lion himself has bred. Sohrab will kill his own father! And when the father is dead, we can easily overcome the insolent son, and send him to his everlasting sleep."

Houman and Barman smiled at their king's clever plan.

"You must go with Sohrab," Afrasyab told them, "but you must keep the secret of his birth well hidden. Neither the father nor the son must know who it is they face. No one must tell Sohrab which of the Iranian warriors is his father."

Sohrab and the White Fortress

There was a white fortress guarding the border of Iran. Its governor was called Hajir. When Hajir saw an army approach from the direction of Turan, led by a huge young warrior astride a great charger, he saddled his own horse and rode out to challenge him.

Sohrab shouted to him, "You fool! Do you really want to throw your life away? Who do you think you are, daring to raise your lance against me? I tell you, your mother will be crying over your body before darkness falls tonight."

Hajir taunted Sohrab in return. "I am Hajir the Brave, the leader of this garrison, and now I'm going to strike the head from your body, and send it to King Kay Kavus with my compliments!"

Sohrab merely smiled at these threats. He spurred on his horse and galloped at Hajir, his lance at the ready. After a short tussle, Hajir was toppled from his charger and lay in the dust. Sohrab flung himself from his own horse and raised his sword, ready to strike Hajir's head from his body, but Hajir rolled to one side, and began to whimper and plead for his life.

Sohrab could not hurt a disarmed man. He spared Hajir's life, but made him his prisoner.

Gordafarid, the Warrior Girl

A girl lived in the White Fortress, the daughter of one of the old heroes of Iran. Her name was Gordafarid. When she heard that the governor of the fortress had grovelled, begging for his life, in front of the enemy's champion, she was filled with rage and shame. She stormed off to the fortress's armoury, dressed herself in a knight's full armour, and bundled her long hair inside a helmet. Then she saddled the fastest horse in the stables and spurred it out through the gates in a furious gallop. She rode straight up to the massed ranks of Sohrab's army, shouting, in a voice of thunder, "Come on, you heroes and warriors! Which of you is going to fight with me?"

She was so fierce that not one Turanian dared to take up her challenge, until at last Sohrab noticed her.

"Aha!" he laughed. "Here's another one who'll fall victim to my sword!"

Quickly, he mounted his own horse and galloped out to attack her. Gordafarid bent her bow, whipped arrows from her quiver, and sent

such a hail of them towards Sohrab that the young hero had to cover his head with his shield. Sohrab charged towards her, and she felt as if a flame of fire was about to devour her. She shook her horse's reins and he reared up as if he wished to jump to the clouds. From this height, she hurled her lance at Sohrab. He dodged the blow but, as fierce as a leopard pouncing on his prey, he struck Gordafarid with his own lance. The tip of it caught her waist and cut through the ties that bound her armour. She reeled back but, undaunted, she drew her sword and with one blow shattered Sohrab's lance. Then she wheeled her horse round and galloped off.

Sohrab chased after her. He let fly his noose. It snaked around her waist. He caught up with her, and snatched the helmet off her head. Her long hair tumbled out of it, falling over her shoulders, and for the first time he saw her lovely face.

"A girl!" he gasped. "No, don't try to escape from me!" And he tightened the noose still further. "If the warriors of Iran are as brave as the girls, they'll send the dust of battle up to the spinning stars."

Gordafarid knew that it was the moment for cunning, if the fortress and all the people in it were to be saved.

"Be careful, hero," she said. "If your army sees that you have been fighting with a girl, they will laugh at you. They'll speak about it for ever more round their camp fires. But no one need know. I won't tell. And there's no need for more killing. We won't attack you again if you will only retire and leave us in peace."

She smiled at him, and Sohrab thought that Paradise could not offer a more beautiful sight. He said cautiously, "Do not try to deceive me. If you break your promise you will see what I shall do! Do not think that the strong walls of your fortress will save you."

But Gordafarid had achieved her aim. She turned her horse's head and galloped back to the fortress with Sohrab by her side. The porters rushed to open the gates, and Gordafarid, weary, covered in blood but triumphant, rode inside.

Within the fortress, the people had been weeping for her, sure that she would be killed. Now her father ran forward and said, "O my brave child! My young lioness! We thought we would never see you alive again. Thank God that you are safe and unhurt! You have saved us all from shame and death."

Gordafarid burst into peals of laughter. She ran up to the ramparts and looked down on the Iranian army. She saw Sohrab looking up at her and couldn't resist calling down to him, "Go back to where you came from, you master of the Asian hordes."

Sohrab was enraged by this taunt. 'I could have taken this fortress easily,' he thought, 'but she has made a fool of me.'

He began to storm at her, threatening to grind the walls of the fortress to dust and catch Gordafarid and punish her severely.

But the girl only smiled as she listened. "You are a great warrior, as I can see," she said, "but there is one who is more powerful than you. When King Kay Kavus hears that an army from Turan has attacked us, he will send Rustam to our aid, and Rustam will tear you to pieces, like a tiger tears his prey. Go home, young warrior, if you want to save your life."

Her words maddened Sohrab even more. He took out his rage by plundering the countryside round the castle.

'It's too late to storm the castle tonight,' he thought. 'But tomorrow they'll learn the lesson that I'm going to teach them!'

That night Gordafarid's father composed a letter to Kay Kavus.

"Come and help us, sire!" he wrote. "A great army has come out of the east, and at its head is a young warrior of such astonishing size and strength that we have never seen his equal. He is as ferocious as a tiger, his voice is like thunder, and though he is a mere boy he has taken prisoner the brave Hajir, our commander, and threatens to kill us all. His name is Sohrab. Surely, he must be of the family of Sam and Zal and Rustam, for there is no one else who could father such a child. Sire, do not wait for more news. Come quickly with your army, before this young giant lays waste the whole of Iran."

A messenger, carrying the letter, slipped out of the fortress and was away across the plains as fast and silently as the wind. Then the entire garrison, and all the able-bodied men, quietly packed up their weapons, their armour and their baggage, and using a secret tunnel, escaped from the fortress, riding away to join the armies of Kay Kavus.

In the morning, Sohrab mounted his horse and led his soldiers out to attack the fortress, but to his surprise there were no armed men on the walls, the gates swung open at his command, and no one came forward to fight.

Sohrab ran through the fortress, hunting high and low for Gordafarid. 'I must find her,' he thought. 'I must see her again. There's no other woman in the world for me.'

> *The hero-boy runs through the fort.*
> *His pride is humbled, his heart is caught.*
> *But the castle is empty. The bird has flown.*
> *Sad Sohrab must remain alone.*

RUSTAM IS SUMMONED

Kay Kavus Sends for Rustam

When news of the invasion reached Kay Kavus, he called his lords and generals together. "What shall we do?" he asked them. "How shall we beat the Turanian hordes back from our borders?"

Everyone urged him to send for Rustam, so Kay Kavus called his scribe and dictated a letter to the hero.

"As soon as you read this letter," wrote the scribe, "whether it arrives by day or by night, do not delay for a second. If you have a rose in your hand, do not pause even to sniff its scent. Open your mouth only to shout your war cry, and ride here in all haste with your cavalry around you. For you are the only man in all the world who can save Iran from this fearful Turanian."

He gave the letter to Giv, Gudarz's noble son. Giv leapt on his horse and rode day and night, pausing neither to eat nor drink, until he arrived at Rustam's home in Zabolistan.

The watchmen on the walls saw in the distance the dust raised by his horse's galloping hooves. "A horseman is coming, as fast as lightning, from the direction of Iran!" they cried.

Rustam rode out to meet Giv. Together they trotted back into Rustam's palace.

When Rustam had read Kay Kavus's letter, and Giv had told him about the mighty young champion invading Iran, he laughed out loud.

"What nonsense!" he said. "No great warrior has ever come out of Turan. I have a son there myself. His mother is a princess of Samangan. She has sent me word that the boy is growing well, but is still only a child. My young lion cub can't possibly be the man who threw Hajir off his horse, and took the White Fortress. We have no need to fear him. Come in, Giv. You must rest. We'll feast together before we set off."

"My orders are to return with you at once," protested Giv.

"Never mind that," said Rustam. "We'll easily send the Turanians packing. We'll march on their army like a vast rolling tide, and their little flame will be snuffed out. When this fiery young fellow sees my banner, he'll turn at once and flee in terror."

Giv gave in to Rustam's persuasion, and for three days the two friends ate and drank, rising late each morning and feasting again each night.

On the fourth day, Giv saddled his horse and prepared to ride away. "Kay Kavus is a hard taskmaster," he said, "and if we delay any longer, he will be furious and seek revenge."

And so, at last, Rustam ordered his trumpeter to sound the advance. Mounting Rakhsh, he rode out at the head of his armoured troops and took the road to Iran.

The Anger of Kay Kavus

Rustam's delay had maddened Kay Kavus. He stalked into the audience chamber where Rustam had at last arrived, and let out a cry of rage at the sight of the champion.

"Who are you to disobey my orders?" he roared. "I tell you, if I had a sword in my hand I would send your head rolling in the dust like an orange. Guards, arrest this man! Take him out and hang him! I never want to see his face again."

"What?" cried Giv, when he heard this. "Sire, this is Rustam! You cannot do such a thing to him!"

"And you, Giv! You're another traitor," bellowed Kay Kavus. "Guards, hang him too!"

Tus stepped forwards and grasped Rustam's arm, but Rustam shook him off, sending the noble general sprawling on the ground.

102

"How can you call yourself a king?" he shouted at Kay Kavus. "Your every action is worse than the last. The armies of Rum, Mazanderan, China, Egypt and Hamaveran have all bowed down before me and my noble Rakhsh. It is thanks to me alone that you are still alive. From now on, I will never come to the aid of Iran again. Save yourself, if you can, from this valiant Turanian who is invading your kingdom!"

He stormed out of the palace, and none dared stand in his way. Mounting Rakhsh, he rode off as fast as a whirlwind. As he went, he cried aloud,

> *"Who is this king, who wishes me dead?*
> *It was I who set the crown on his head!*
> *My helmet's my crown; Rakhsh is my throne.*
> *In peace or in war I surrender to none."*

The Iranians trembled to see Rustam go. "Our foolish king has no sense or decency," they said to each other. "He owes his life to Rustam, and this is how he treats him. We must go to Kay Kavus, and make him see reason."

Gudarz offered to speak to the king. "Sire," he said, "tell us what crime Rustam has committed. Why did you threaten to hang him? Have you forgotten how he saved you from the demons of Mazanderan, and the King of Hamaveran? Who can now deliver you from this wolf who is howling on the borders of your kingdom?"

Kay Kavus was humbled by his words. "You are right," he said. "I was hasty. Go after Rustam. Tell him that I am biting my hands with shame. Persuade him to come back to me."

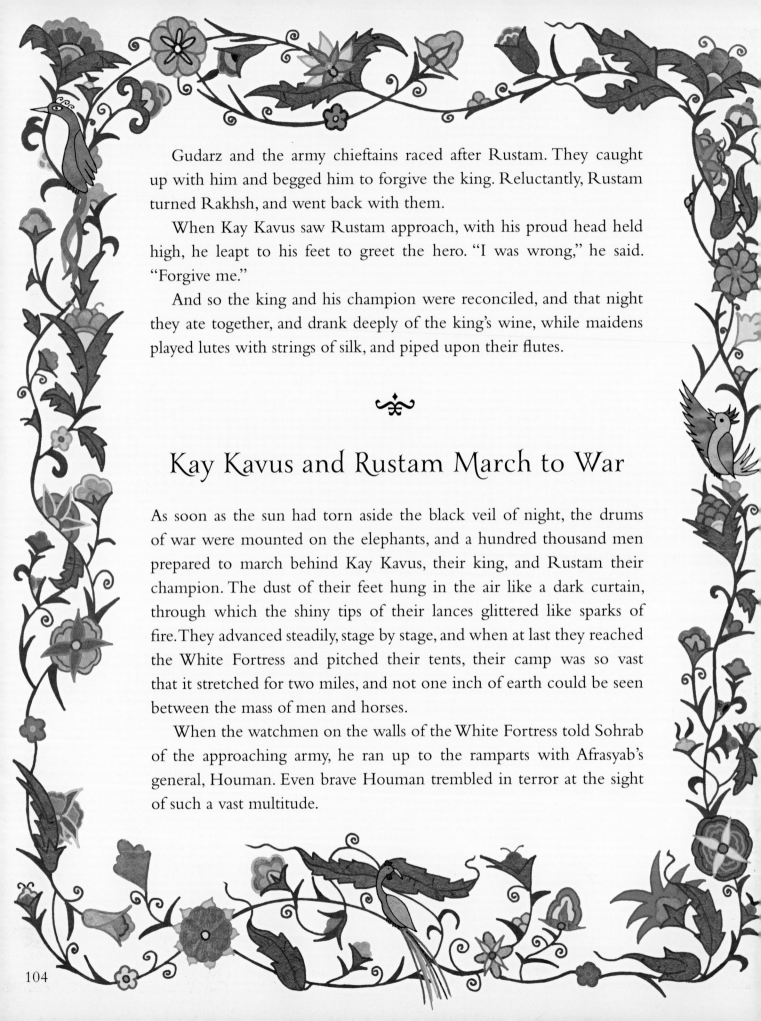

Gudarz and the army chieftains raced after Rustam. They caught up with him and begged him to forgive the king. Reluctantly, Rustam turned Rakhsh, and went back with them.

When Kay Kavus saw Rustam approach, with his proud head held high, he leapt to his feet to greet the hero. "I was wrong," he said. "Forgive me."

And so the king and his champion were reconciled, and that night they ate together, and drank deeply of the king's wine, while maidens played lutes with strings of silk, and piped upon their flutes.

Kay Kavus and Rustam March to War

As soon as the sun had torn aside the black veil of night, the drums of war were mounted on the elephants, and a hundred thousand men prepared to march behind Kay Kavus, their king, and Rustam their champion. The dust of their feet hung in the air like a dark curtain, through which the shiny tips of their lances glittered like sparks of fire. They advanced steadily, stage by stage, and when at last they reached the White Fortress and pitched their tents, their camp was so vast that it stretched for two miles, and not one inch of earth could be seen between the mass of men and horses.

When the watchmen on the walls of the White Fortress told Sohrab of the approaching army, he ran up to the ramparts with Afrasyab's general, Houman. Even brave Houman trembled in terror at the sight of such a vast multitude.

"What are you afraid of?" scoffed Sohrab. "In all this mass of men there is not one who can stand up against me in battle. You will see, Houman. You will see."

And with a smile on his lips, he ran down the steps and called for a goblet of wine.

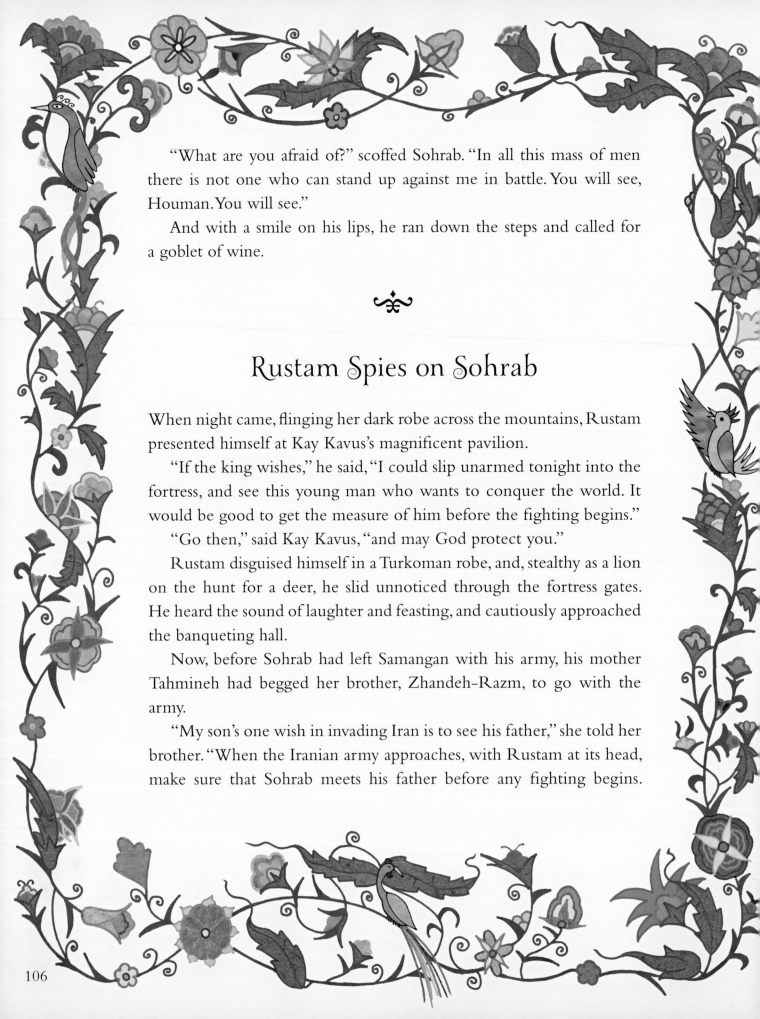

Rustam Spies on Sohrab

When night came, flinging her dark robe across the mountains, Rustam presented himself at Kay Kavus's magnificent pavilion.

"If the king wishes," he said, "I could slip unarmed tonight into the fortress, and see this young man who wants to conquer the world. It would be good to get the measure of him before the fighting begins."

"Go then," said Kay Kavus, "and may God protect you."

Rustam disguised himself in a Turkoman robe, and, stealthy as a lion on the hunt for a deer, he slid unnoticed through the fortress gates. He heard the sound of laughter and feasting, and cautiously approached the banqueting hall.

Now, before Sohrab had left Samangan with his army, his mother Tahmineh had begged her brother, Zhandeh-Razm, to go with the army.

"My son's one wish in invading Iran is to see his father," she told her brother. "When the Iranian army approaches, with Rustam at its head, make sure that Sohrab meets his father before any fighting begins.

Afrasyab has ordered that no one should point Rustam out to the boy. You must disobey him, so that no harm comes to my son."

Rustam slipped into the banqueting hall and watched from the shadows. He saw Sohrab sitting on a throne. The boy was taller than any man. His massive arms were crossed on his lion-like chest, and his eyes flashed fire. Around him sat his young men, praising their leader, while fifty servants ran to do his bidding.

"How strange!" thought Rustam. "This young man is the image of my noble grandfather, Sam."

After a while Sohrab's uncle, Zhandeh-Razm, came out of the banqueting hall and walked past the place where Rustam stood. He was surprised to see such a tall, noble-looking stranger standing there.

"Who are you?" he demanded. "What are you doing here? Come out into the light so that I can see you."

Sensing that he was about to be unmasked, Rustam lifted one mighty arm and struck Zhandeh-Razm on the neck. The man fell like a stone, dead, at Rustam's feet. Rustam turned, and went swiftly away, out of the fortress.

A little later, Sohrab noticed that Zhandeh-Razm had not returned. "Where is my uncle?" he asked. "Why hasn't he come back?"

His men went outside to look, and found Zhandeh-Razm lying lifeless on the ground. They let out cries of horror, and Sohrab came running to see what had happened.

"A wolf has been here among us," he cried, "creeping in to kill. With the help of God, I'll make the Iranians pay for this."

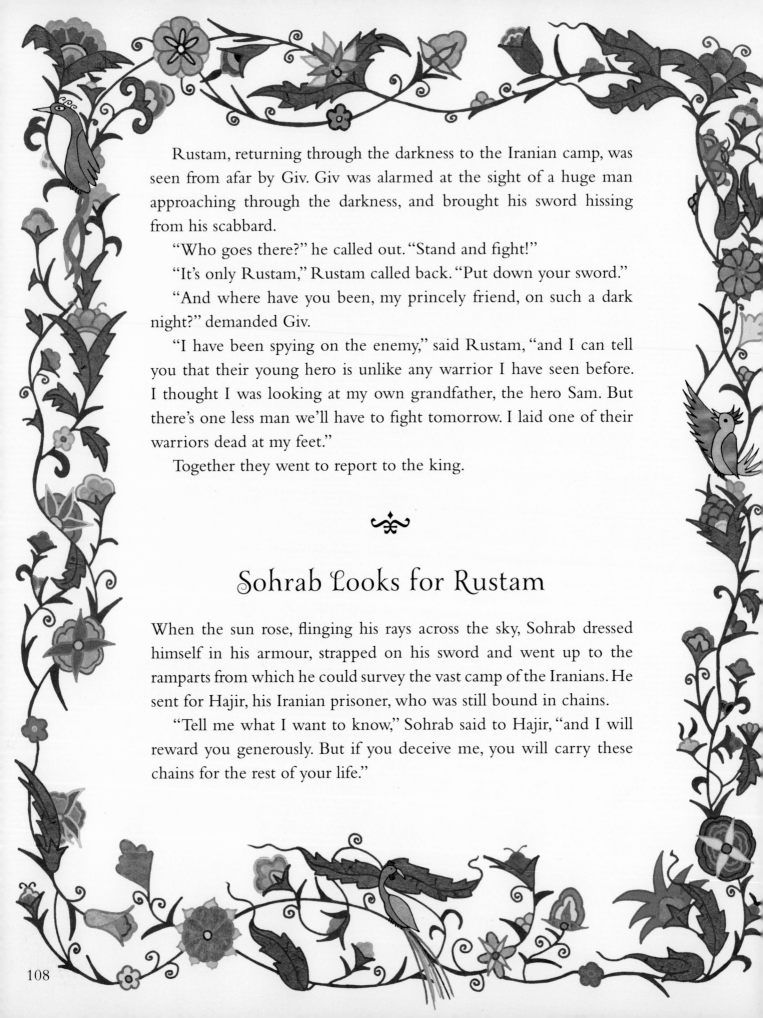

Rustam, returning through the darkness to the Iranian camp, was seen from afar by Giv. Giv was alarmed at the sight of a huge man approaching through the darkness, and brought his sword hissing from his scabbard.

"Who goes there?" he called out. "Stand and fight!"

"It's only Rustam," Rustam called back. "Put down your sword."

"And where have you been, my princely friend, on such a dark night?" demanded Giv.

"I have been spying on the enemy," said Rustam, "and I can tell you that their young hero is unlike any warrior I have seen before. I thought I was looking at my own grandfather, the hero Sam. But there's one less man we'll have to fight tomorrow. I laid one of their warriors dead at my feet."

Together they went to report to the king.

❧

Sohrab Looks for Rustam

When the sun rose, flinging his rays across the sky, Sohrab dressed himself in his armour, strapped on his sword and went up to the ramparts from which he could survey the vast camp of the Iranians. He sent for Hajir, his Iranian prisoner, who was still bound in chains.

"Tell me what I want to know," Sohrab said to Hajir, "and I will reward you generously. But if you deceive me, you will carry these chains for the rest of your life."

"I will tell you everything you wish," said Hajir.

"Then look," said Sohrab, and he pointed to a magnificent pavilion, coloured like the rainbow. A hundred elephants stood waiting outside it, and a purple banner, embroidered with a golden sun and moon, fluttered in the breeze above a turquoise throne. "Whose tent is that, Hajir, and who has the right to sit upon that throne?"

"It belongs to Kay Kavus, the King of Iran," said Hajir. "And he has lions as well as elephants in his train."

"To the right of the king's camp, over there," Sohrab went on. "Do you see that black pavilion, surrounded by soldiers? Behind it are countless smaller tents, and above them flies a banner bearing the device of an elephant, which is guarded by soldiers wearing boots of gold."

"That is the camp of Tus, the son of Nozar," answered Hajir.

"Well then," persisted Sohrab, "whose is that red pavilion, pitched under a golden banner, blazoned with a lion, round which surges a mass of armed men carrying lances?"

"That belongs to the hero Gudarz, the father of Giv," said Hajir. "He is the destroyer of armies. He has eighty sons as valiant as himself. Not even a crocodile, a tiger of the desert or a leopard of the mountains would dare to fight with him."

Sohrab scanned the camp again, longing to hear only one name on Hajir's lips.

"Look carefully!" he cried. "Do you see that green tent there? Above it floats the leather banner of Kaveh the blacksmith. Under it, on a noble throne, sits a man bigger by far than all the rest,

while in front of him stands a gigantic horse, tossing his head and neighing to his master. Elephants clad in battle armour surround them. I have never seen such a man, or such a horse. Look at his emblem! It shows a dragon, and on the tip of its staff sits a golden lion."

Hajir said to himself, "If I tell this young firebrand that the hero he sees is Rustam himself, he will single him out and fall upon him, and if he wins, the Iranians will turn and flee."

Aloud he said, "It is some lord of Tartary, who has recently joined the king. I don't know his name."

Sohrab had recognised, one after the other, the signs of his father which his mother had carefully taught him. He pressed Hajir to tell him more, but Hajir would say nothing, and Sohrab did not believe his own eyes. His heart sank with disappointment. He turned away from Rustam, while Hajir pointed out Giv, with his banner of a wolf's head, and the white pavilion of Prince Fariborz, the son of Kay Kavus, and the scarlet pavilion with the wild-boar banner of Goraz of the family of Giv, never saying the name which Sohrab longed to hear.

Sohrab's eyes fastened again on the huge warrior beneath the green banner, and the golden horse with the great noose coiled round his neck.

"Why, among all these champions, have you not mentioned Rustam, the greatest of them all?" he cried despairingly. "You told me that he is the commander of the army and the guardian of the frontiers of Iran. Kay Kavus himself has come out against me, with all his lords and generals. Where is Rustam, who always rides out at the head of the army, when the thunder of battle echoes round the land?"

"I tell you," insisted Hajir, "I don't know where Rustam is. Perhaps he has returned to Zabolistan to celebrate the Spring Festival."

"How dare you?" shouted Sohrab. "Would the great Rustam leave every other champion of Iran to come out with their king, and stay at home to enjoy a festival? If he did such a thing, everyone would laugh at him. I beg you, Hajir, show me Rustam! If you do, I will heap treasures upon you. If you do not, you'll pay for it with your life."

But Hajir thought, 'The great Rustam is growing old, and this young man is a champion such as I have never seen. If he kills the hero of Iran, he will seize the throne of Kay Kavus and throw all Iran into turmoil. I must not reveal the truth. Death is better than dishonour.'

"Why are you so impatient?" he said at last. "I've told you what I know. You should be thankful that Rustam isn't here, for if you were to meet him on the field of battle, he would utterly destroy you."

Tahmineh taught her son to know
The signs his father's camp would show:
The dragon flag, the golden horse,
The giant man of matchless force.
Sohrab sees, but listens to the lies
And does not trust the sight of his own eyes.

THE BATTLE OF SOHRAB AND RUSTAM

Sohrab Makes his Challenge

Maddened by disappointment, Sohrab lashed out at Hajir and struck him to the ground. Then he prepared himself for war, putting on his coat of mail, and strapping on his breastplate and helmet. Anger boiled in his veins. He picked up his lance, his noose, his bow and his mace, leaped on his horse, shouted a war cry and burst out of the fortress like a raging lion, burning for the fight. He launched himself straight at the pavilion of Kay Kavus, ripping the awning which covered it with the point of his lance. His attack was so furious that the king's warriors scattered in front of him.

"This young giant is like a raging elephant," they said to each other. "Only a madman would dare to fight him."

Sohrab began to shout taunts at Kay Kavus. "Do you call yourself a king?" he bellowed. "You have never won a fight in single combat. Is there not one in your whole army who is man enough to fight me?"

He waited, dancing with impatience, but no one dared to respond. Sohrab swung his lance again, sending seventy tent pegs flying out of the ground so that half the king's great pavilion collapsed.

Trembling with fear, Kay Kavus called out, "Send for Rustam! Not one of my own men dares to face this roaring lion. Rustam alone can save us!"

Tus ran swiftly to Rustam's camp.

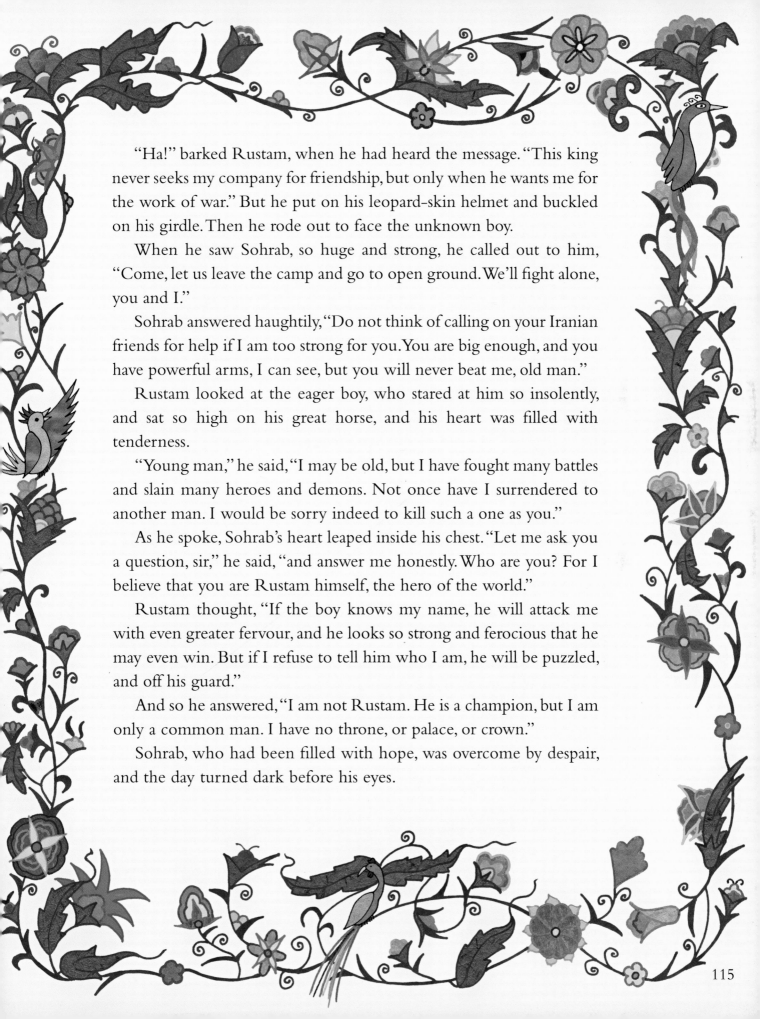

"Ha!" barked Rustam, when he had heard the message. "This king never seeks my company for friendship, but only when he wants me for the work of war." But he put on his leopard-skin helmet and buckled on his girdle. Then he rode out to face the unknown boy.

When he saw Sohrab, so huge and strong, he called out to him, "Come, let us leave the camp and go to open ground. We'll fight alone, you and I."

Sohrab answered haughtily, "Do not think of calling on your Iranian friends for help if I am too strong for you. You are big enough, and you have powerful arms, I can see, but you will never beat me, old man."

Rustam looked at the eager boy, who stared at him so insolently, and sat so high on his great horse, and his heart was filled with tenderness.

"Young man," he said, "I may be old, but I have fought many battles and slain many heroes and demons. Not once have I surrendered to another man. I would be sorry indeed to kill such a one as you."

As he spoke, Sohrab's heart leaped inside his chest. "Let me ask you a question, sir," he said, "and answer me honestly. Who are you? For I believe that you are Rustam himself, the hero of the world."

Rustam thought, "If the boy knows my name, he will attack me with even greater fervour, and he looks so strong and ferocious that he may even win. But if I refuse to tell him who I am, he will be puzzled, and off his guard."

And so he answered, "I am not Rustam. He is a champion, but I am only a common man. I have no throne, or palace, or crown."

Sohrab, who had been filled with hope, was overcome by despair, and the day turned dark before his eyes.

The First Battle Between Sohrab and Rustam

Sohrab and Rustam went to the battle ground and hurled javelins at each other. When their metal tips were blunted, they pulled out their swords and rushed forward, hacking fiercely, until sparks flew from the blades, which shattered at last through the force of their blows. Then each one took his heavy mace and swung it high, but even the mighty arms of both the giant man and the colossal boy were exhausted by the violence of their attacks, while their two horses stood trembling with the effort, their heads drooping.

What cruel fate has played this trick?
Rustam afraid, Sohrab heartsick.
Filled with pride from battles won,
The father tries to slay his son.
Where is the love they owe each other?
How can the son not know his father?

At last they drew apart. Rustam was filled with dread. Sohrab was overcome with sorrow.

Rustam said to himself, 'Even my battle with the White Devil was a game compared to this, and now my courage is failing. This boy is no famous warrior, or hero of renown, but he matches me blow for blow.'

And he was ashamed of his weakness.

When the horses had had time to rest for a while, Sohrab and Rustam took up their bows and sent their arrows flying, but the old

116

hero's tiger-skin tunic and the young man's coat of mail protected them and the arrows did no harm. They threw down their weapons, and coming close together, tried to grasp each other by the belt, each wanting to unseat his adversary from his horse and throw him to the ground. But Rustam was unmovable, and Sohrab sat as firm as rock in his saddle. Rustam, who had often lifted huge boulders in one hand, could not dislodge him by an inch.

At last Sohrab picked up his mace again and struck Rustam a mighty blow on his shoulder.

Rustam tried to hide his pain, but Sohrab saw it and said mockingly, "See, old man, how you stagger under my blow!"

Frustrated, each of them wheeled away from the battle ground. Rustam, like a tiger pursuing his prey, spurred Rakhsh towards the Turanian camp, slashing right and left at the enemy with his sword. Sohrab galloped furiously into the camp of the Iranians, and all fell in terror before him.

When Rustam saw what he was doing, he roared like a lion, raced after him and shouted, "You bloodthirsty madman! How dare you run wild here, like a wolf among the sheep?"

Sohrab answered, "You attacked us first, though none in our camp challenged you."

They glared at each other.

Rustam said, "Night is falling. Let us draw back now. Tomorrow, on the battle field, we'll fight again. For one of us there will be death and for the other glory. It shall be as God wills."

Sohrab and Rustam Return to their Camps

In the Turanian camp, Afrasyab's general, Houman, was waiting for Sohrab.

Sohrab said to him, "Leopards and tigers have fallen to my sword, but this old man is more powerful than any of them. Tomorrow, though, you will see, Houman. I'll draw down the fire of heaven with the tip of my lance. Now bring me food and wine and let us feast tonight."

In the Iranian camp, Rustam sought out Kay Kavus.

"Never have I seen so young a boy possessed of such wild courage," he told the king. "Tomorrow I will pit myself against him with all my strength. The Creator of the sun and moon will decide who is to be the victor."

He returned to his pavilion, and said to his men, "If I fall tomorrow, don't mourn for me. Return quietly to Zabolistan and comfort my mother and father, who still live. Stay loyal to the king and serve him faithfully, as I have tried to do. This is the life I have chosen. Whoever puts spurs on his heels and makes his horse charge into battle, knocks on the gates of death."

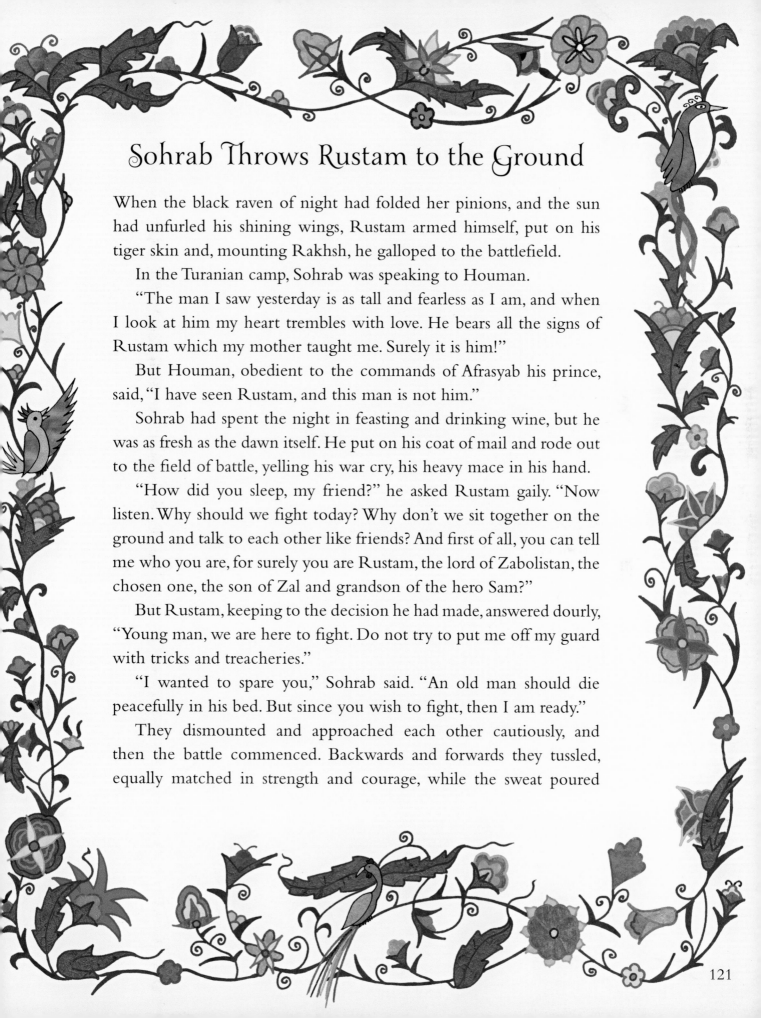

Sohrab Throws Rustam to the Ground

When the black raven of night had folded her pinions, and the sun had unfurled his shining wings, Rustam armed himself, put on his tiger skin and, mounting Rakhsh, he galloped to the battlefield.

In the Turanian camp, Sohrab was speaking to Houman.

"The man I saw yesterday is as tall and fearless as I am, and when I look at him my heart trembles with love. He bears all the signs of Rustam which my mother taught me. Surely it is him!"

But Houman, obedient to the commands of Afrasyab his prince, said, "I have seen Rustam, and this man is not him."

Sohrab had spent the night in feasting and drinking wine, but he was as fresh as the dawn itself. He put on his coat of mail and rode out to the field of battle, yelling his war cry, his heavy mace in his hand.

"How did you sleep, my friend?" he asked Rustam gaily. "Now listen. Why should we fight today? Why don't we sit together on the ground and talk to each other like friends? And first of all, you can tell me who you are, for surely you are Rustam, the lord of Zabolistan, the chosen one, the son of Zal and grandson of the hero Sam?"

But Rustam, keeping to the decision he had made, answered dourly, "Young man, we are here to fight. Do not try to put me off my guard with tricks and treacheries."

"I wanted to spare you," Sohrab said. "An old man should die peacefully in his bed. But since you wish to fight, then I am ready."

They dismounted and approached each other cautiously, and then the battle commenced. Backwards and forwards they tussled, equally matched in strength and courage, while the sweat poured from their bodies. At last, Sohrab grasped Rustam by the belt, lifted him high and dashed him to the ground. He pulled out his dagger, ready to sever the hero's head with one blow.

But the wily Rustam, seeing the danger he was in, fell back on cunning to save himself.

"Listen, my young champion," he said. "Don't disgrace yourself. According to the laws of chivalry, you should not kill your enemy at his first fall but let him rise and wrestle again. It is only at the second fall that you may take your knife and end it."

Sohrab, eager to be a man of honour, stood back, believing in his youthful innocence that Rustam had told the truth. He let Rustam go. Then, still filled with boundless energy, he rode cheerfully into the nearby field and began to chase the gazelles grazing there.

Houman suddenly appeared through the cloud of dust which Sohrab's horse had raised. When he heard how Sohrab had had Rustam at his mercy, and had let him go, he burst out, "You young fool! How easily he tricked you! You'll regret this foolish action, you'll see."

Furious and ashamed, Sohrab returned to the Turanian camp.

As soon as Sohrab had released him, Rustam leaped to his feet, like a dead man returning to life. He went to a nearby stream, drank water and washed the dust from his face and body.

Men say that when Rustam was young, God gave him a body of such extraordinary weight that at every step he took, his feet sank into the very rocks, and he had asked God to lighten him so that he could walk with ease. But now, as he felt the hour of exreme danger approach, he begged God to return to him the mighty powers of his youth, and God heard his prayer.

When he had finished praying, he stood back from the stream and returned to the battlefield, his heart troubled and his face pale.

Sohrab was there already. He was charging about in a state of furious anger, his horse rearing under him, tearing up clods of earth with his iron hooves.

And so the great battle began again.

> *One now will live, and one to darkness go.*
> *There's no escape, for God has willed it so.*

The Final Battle

Sohrab and Rustam dismounted and tethered their horses. They stood facing each other.

And now Rustam was possessed of a power so great that he took hold of Sohrab with ease, and bent him backwards towards the ground. The boy felt his adversary's gigantic strength, and his own strength began to slip away. Rustam threw him to the ground. He took out his dagger. He thrust it into Sohrab's chest.

The battle was over.

Sohrab knew that his end was near.

"It was my fault," he whispered. "God made me the warrior that I am, and it is He who has struck me down. You are innocent of my death. I did what I have done only because I wanted to see my father.

I longed for him. And it was all for nothing. I will never meet him now. But listen, stranger! When my father hears how you have killed me, don't try to run away! Even if you disguise yourself as a star, and hide among the galaxies of heaven, my father will find you. He will revenge my death. Someone will tell him. Someone will go to Rustam, and describe to him how you threw his son Sohrab on the ground and killed him."

When Rustam heard this, he stared aghast at the boy bleeding at his feet. The world swam before his eyes. Then he let out a terrible cry of grief and despair.

"But I am Rustam!" he cried. "Can this be true? Are you Sohrab, my son?"

Sohrab started up, then fell back, as weakness overcame him.

"You are Rustam? Oh, why did you not tell me when I asked you? Why did I not recognise you? I tried to stop our fight, but you would not listen to me. I looked, but saw no sign of love in you. Take off my armour. There! Can you see? My mother put this onyx

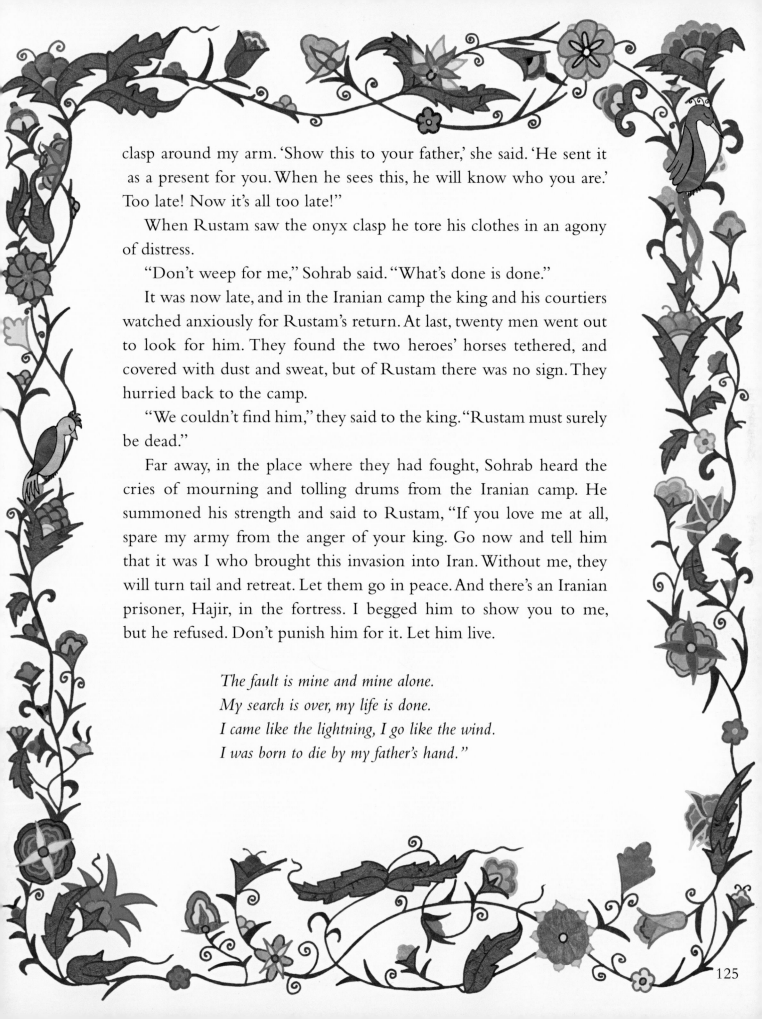

clasp around my arm. 'Show this to your father,' she said. 'He sent it as a present for you. When he sees this, he will know who you are.' Too late! Now it's all too late!"

When Rustam saw the onyx clasp he tore his clothes in an agony of distress.

"Don't weep for me," Sohrab said. "What's done is done."

It was now late, and in the Iranian camp the king and his courtiers watched anxiously for Rustam's return. At last, twenty men went out to look for him. They found the two heroes' horses tethered, and covered with dust and sweat, but of Rustam there was no sign. They hurried back to the camp.

"We couldn't find him," they said to the king. "Rustam must surely be dead."

Far away, in the place where they had fought, Sohrab heard the cries of mourning and tolling drums from the Iranian camp. He summoned his strength and said to Rustam, "If you love me at all, spare my army from the anger of your king. Go now and tell him that it was I who brought this invasion into Iran. Without me, they will turn tail and retreat. Let them go in peace. And there's an Iranian prisoner, Hajir, in the fortress. I begged him to show you to me, but he refused. Don't punish him for it. Let him live.

> *The fault is mine and mine alone.*
> *My search is over, my life is done.*
> *I came like the lightning, I go like the wind.*
> *I was born to die by my father's hand."*

Sorrow had ripped the breath from Rustam's chest. His heart was on fire. Tears streamed from his eyes. He ran to Rakhsh, burning to obey Sohrab's last request, and galloped to the Iranian camp to forestall their attack on Sohrab's army. Then he wheeled round and raced back to his dying son, with the lords of Iran at his heels.

The sight of Sohrab, so near death, and drenched in the blood which he had spilled, filled Rustam with such new anguish that he seized his dagger, ready to cut his own throat. His friends leaped forwards and disarmed him.

"He still lives!" they said. "Look! He breathes! He may recover!"

A wild hope surged in Rustam's breast. "The elixir!" he cried. "King Kavus holds in his treasure chest a miraculous medicine that heals all wounds! Ride, one of you, ride! Tell the king that if ever he would thank me for the service I have given him, he should send me the elixir, with a cup of wine, and save the life of Sohrab."

Gudarz, the father of Giv, rode like the wind to Kay Kavus.

But the king's face lengthened as he listened. Slowly, he shook his head.

"You heard how Rustam insulted me. 'Who is Kay Kavus?' he said insolently, in front of my whole court. 'It was I who set the crown on your head!' Rustam is too powerful and rebellious already, and if he is joined by a son as valiant as himself, the pair of them will turn on me and snatch my throne for themselves."

Sickened by the king's malice and ingratitude, Gudarz rode back to the place where Sohrab lay. "The king is as hard as stone," he told Rustam. "He refuses to help you. Go to him yourself. Perhaps you can melt his icy heart."

The Grief of Rustam

Rustam made his servants spread out a cloth of gold by a flower-fringed stream, and gently laid his wounded son upon it. But as he set off to plead with the king, a messenger ran after him.

"Your son is dead! He is dead!" the man cried. "He looked round for you, and saw you were not there, then he gave a last sigh, and his soul flew from his body."

Rustam flung himself to the ground. "O my son, my son Sohrab!" he cried. "No one in all the world was equal to you. There was no one I would have loved like you. What have I done? How shall I tell your mother? Did ever a father commit such a terrible crime? I shall be cursed for ever more. O Sohrab, my son!"

He made them cover the boy's body with the silk of royalty, and they carried Sohrab away from the battlefield to his father's pavilion. There they lit a great fire and threw into it Rustam's tents of many-coloured silks, and his leopard-skin saddle, which he had been used to sit upon as if it was a throne.

And the lords of Iran sat with Rustam in the dust, and tried to comfort him, but they could not.

The Death of Rustam

Kay Kavus ordered his army to retreat and Tus, Gudarz and Giv led the troops back to Iran, but Rustam and his men returned to their home in Zabolistan. They docked the tails of their black horses and smashed their cymbals and drums. They marched in solemn silence before the coffin.

Rustam himself refused to ride, but walked on foot, his clothes torn to rags, his heart broken.

A messenger had ridden ahead to tell Zal the dreadful news. The old man rode out to meet his son, and great was his grief.

Rustam built for Sohrab a magnificent tomb.

Far away, in Samangan, Tahmineh had been watching the road anxiously for her son's return. When a messenger rode hot-foot to tell her that he was dead, she became mad with sorrow.

"O my young lion, you wanted only to find your father. Why did you not tell him that you were his son? I should have followed you on your quest! I would have made sure that you came to no harm!"

Tahmineh lived on for a single year, and at the end of it she died, freeing her soul to rejoin her son for all eternity.

Rustam lived for many more years, and he died in the same hour and in the same manner as his beloved horse, Rakhsh, his best friend in death as he had been in life.

Here ends the story of Sohrab and how he died at the hand of his father, Rustam. And the poet, pausing from his task, looks out at us, and says:

"Oh little man, forget your pride.
Your hour of death God will decide.
What lies beyond the grave we cannot know.
Accept your fate, for it is written so."

Main Characters in the Shahnameh

Kayumars
Hushang
Tahmuras
Jamshid   **Kings of Iran**
Feridun
Kay Kobad
Kay Kavus

Faranak   **Feridun's mother**

Sam
Zal   **Champions of Iran**
Rustam

Rudabeh   **Zal's wife**

Tahmineh   **Rustam's wife**

Sohrab   **Rustam's son**

Gudarz
Giv, Gudarz's son   **Generals of the Iranian army**
Tus

Ahriman	**A wicked devil**
Mirdas	**The King of Arabia**
Zahhak	**Mirdas's evil son**
Arnavaz and Shahnavaz	**Zahhak's wives**
Kaveh	**A brave blacksmith**
Mehrab	**The King of Kabul**
Afrasyab	**A Turanian prince, the enemy of Iran**
Houman and Barman	**Afrasyab's generals**
Ulad	**A noble young warrior**
Sudabeh	**A princess of Hamaveran**
Hajir	**Governor of the White Fortress**
Gordafarid	**The courageous daughter of an old Iranian hero**
Zhandeh-Razm	**Sohrab's uncle**
Rakhsh	**Rustam's noble horse**
The Simurgh	**A giant magical bird**

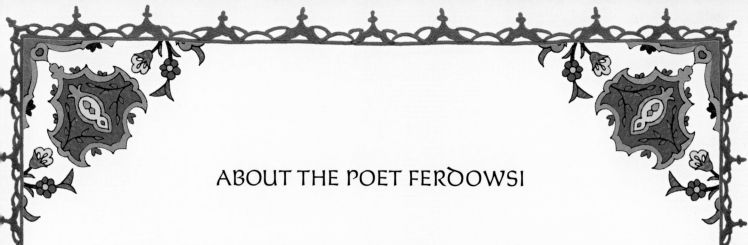

ABOUT THE POET FERDOWSI

Ferdowsi, the poet who wrote the *Shahnameh*, lived more than a thousand years ago. He was the greatest of Iran's great writers and he is revered above them all.

There are many stories about the life of Ferdowsi, but no one really knows the truth about him. One writer said that he had a dearly loved daughter. He wanted to give her a splendid dowry when she married, and so he set about writing his great poem. It took Ferdowsi thirty years to finish his work, so his daughter must have been married long before he finished it.

The *Shahnameh* is a very long poem with 60,000 couplets (pairs of lines of verse). Only a few of the many stories it contains have been retold in this book.

When Ferdowsi had finished writing his poem at last, he took it to the Sultan, hoping to be paid the 60,000 gold coins (one for each couplet) he had been promised, but the Sultan had become prejudiced against him, and Ferdowsi was given only a small sum of money. Disappointed and furious, he stormed off and went to live in Mazanderan.

The Sultan was sorry in the end that he had behaved so badly, and sent camels laden with gifts for Ferdowsi, but the payment came too late. Ferdowsi had died.

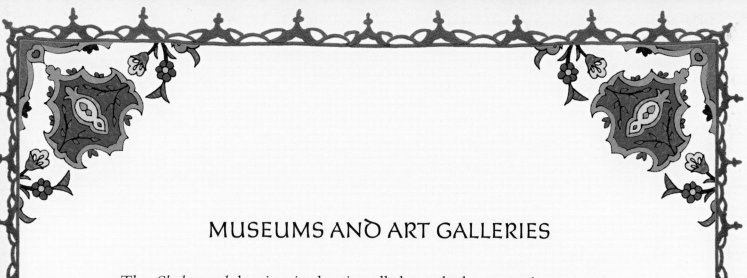

MUSEUMS AND ART GALLERIES

The *Shahnameh* has inspired artists all through the centuries to create exquisitely illustrated manuscripts. You can see examples in many museums and art galleries around the world. Here are some of the most famous:

Canada:	Royal Ontario Museum, Toronto
France:	The Louvre, Paris
Germany:	Museum für Islamische Kunst, Berlin
Iran:	Reza-yi Abbasi Museum, Teheran
Ireland:	The Chester Beatty Library, Dublin
United Kingdom:	The British Library, London
	The Fitzwilliam Museum, Cambridge
United States:	The Metropolitan Museum of Art, New York
	The County Museum of Art, Los Angeles
	The Freer Gallery, Washington DC
	The Sackler Gallery, Washingon DC